POETRY AND THE
CRITICISM OF LIFE

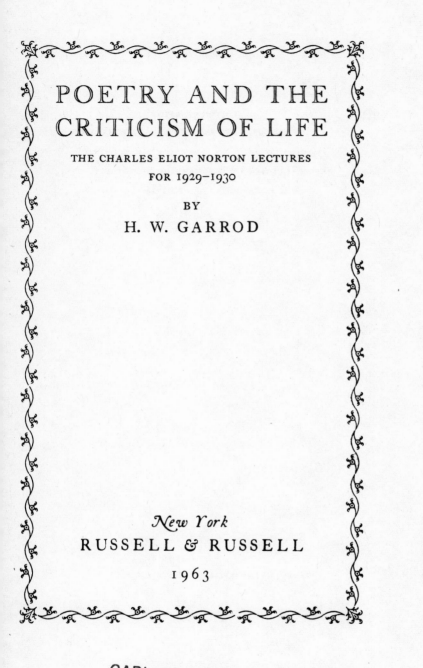

POETRY AND THE CRITICISM OF LIFE

THE CHARLES ELIOT NORTON LECTURES
FOR 1929–1930

BY

H. W. GARROD

New York
RUSSELL & RUSSELL

1963

TO

JOHN LIVINGSTON LOWES

PREFACE

THROUGHOUT this book "Cambridge" means Cambridge, Massachusetts, and "Oxford" means Oxford, England.

Either city is the seat of a great university; and in both these universities there is — what no other university has — a Professorship of Poetry. Passing, as it was my good fortune to do, from the one Professorship to the other, I was anxious to find, for the subject of my Lectures in Cambridge, persons and causes which had connexions with both universities. Three of the Lectures here printed concern themselves with Matthew Arnold — I did not know how I could better illustrate the meaning and purpose of a Professorship of Poetry. Moreover, Matthew Arnold had himself lectured in Cambridge; and he had been a friend of Charles Eliot Norton, in whose memory the Harvard Professorship is founded. With Arnold, it was natural that I should conjoin Emerson and Clough, both of them, like Arnold, friends of Norton, and having, both of them, special associations with Cambridge.

The first and the last of the Lectures plead a cause no longer fashionable, I fancy, either in Oxford or in Cambridge; but a cause which interested profoundly all the great writers whom I have named — with his lifelong championship of the Moral Muse Arnold's fame is especially bound up.

Of the creations of the Moral Muse, Mr. Bridges'
Testament of Beauty is the latest-born, and among
the most lovely. The greatness of this poem seemed
to me to be either missed in America or not justly
apprehended. When I lectured upon it, Mr. Bridges
was still living; and it was but a year or two since
that he visited Harvard and received there an honor-
ary doctorate. The Lecture upon the *Testament of
Beauty* I have felt, therefore, to have a proper place in
this volume.

The Note which accompanies the first paragraph of
the lecture on Clough I owe to the kindness of
Dr. H. S. White, Emeritus Professor of German in
Harvard University.

H. W. G.

CONTENTS

❖❖❖❖❖❖❖❖❖❖❖❖❖❖❖❖❖❖❖❖❖❖

POETRY AND THE
CRITICISM OF LIFE

WIDE as the world is, there are but two Chairs of Poetry in it; and that a man should pass from the one to the other of them might well seem to mark him down for some envy of the gods. At least it should admonish him to walk humbly, to suspect himself, to remember that he is but prose. Five-and-thirty years ago, if I had been asked what the world could give me that I wanted, I think I should have answered, "the Chair of Poetry in Oxford." And if I had been asked, "And after that, what?" I should have said, "Why, nothing." And certainly, in the autumn of 1928, I was not conscious of wanting anything in the world, unless it were wisdom. There were books that I still wanted to read — and to write. But I could have named no office or place of honour that I coveted or that was likely to tempt me if it came my way. It is hard to know oneself; but truly I can think of no preferment which would have tempted me at that time save this one — this other Chair of Poetry, this Harvard Chair offered to an Oxford man. I could hardly misinterpret, let me say, the meaning of the offer. You had the whole world to choose from; and I am not so foolish as not to know that, when your choice lighted upon me, I owed it, not to myself, but to the accident of my connexion with the Chair of Poetry in Oxford. I am more than content that it should be so; and I only wish that I represented better than I do the tradition of that Chair, that I could better sing the song of it in a strange land.

I say "a strange land." Yet I should not be here at all if I had not known that no Englishman who comes here is allowed to feel himself a stranger. If you will forgive me for saying so, that is one of our troubles — we are never treated as strangers, and, as a consequence, we invariably go away knowing all about America. Twice before I have been in the United States; on each occasion for a period of about three months. I sometimes think that I must be the only Englishman who has spent six months in America without knowing all about it — I have never even written a book about it. I come here now, I must suppose, as a teacher. But I am more impressed, as the result of having been here twice before, by the thought of how much I have to learn, how much to unlearn. When I came here before, at least I unlearned a good deal; for I came here at a season when all the world was unlearning most of what it had believed. I came first in the month in which the United States entered the War. No Englishman who was here at that time could go away as foolish as he came, nor fail to take home with him memories precious and abiding. Those were not times of literary leisure; and it was not my fault, therefore, that, though I spent a good many days in Boston, I never so much as set foot within the gates of Harvard. Two of those days, however, stand out in my recollection: the one when, lunching in Boston, I had for my next neighbour a

great man, the late President Eliot, and heard him
make a speech which had for its theme the community
of ideals which binds the English and American
peoples; the other a day which I stole from my official
duties in order to make a pilgrimage to Emerson's
home in Concord. I mention that pilgrimage because
one of the reasons why I cannot feel myself wholly a
stranger here is that Boston and Cambridge have always meant to me Emerson, and of my youth — if I
may say it, and yet claim to have had one — Emerson
was one of the prophets.   Forty-six years ago, almost to a day, Matthew Arnold lectured upon Emerson in Boston. I still recall vividly my first reading of
that lecture; for it first led me to Emerson. I do not
know that Emerson's place in the literature of the
world has been anywhere better indicated than in the
sentences in which, placing him with Marcus Aurelius, Matthew Arnold speaks of him as the "friend
and aider of those who would live in the spirit." Matthew Arnold and Emerson met, so far as I know, only
once; in 1848, and, as I suppose, in Oxford, when
Emerson was the guest of Arnold's friend Clough at
Oriel — Arnold had only just ceased to be a fellow of
Oriel. "A very pleasant interview," Matthew Arnold
says; but he did not like the way in which Emerson
spoke of Wordsworth. I do not know whether he
liked the way in which Wordsworth spoke of Emerson. To Wordsworth, Emerson was a second edition
of Carlyle, somewhat enlarged, but in no way im-
proved; and at least one of his letters characterises
Emerson in terms singularly unsympathetic. Clough,

at a later date, knew Emerson well; and Matthew Arnold, in 1883, got to know both Emerson's family and the great figures of the Emerson circle. Both poets were the friends of that distinguished man of letters in whose honour this Chair was founded — this Harvard Professorship of Poetry.

When I was a professor at Oxford, it meant much to me that I sat in the seat of Matthew Arnold, a great poet, a great critic, a great "friend and aider of those who would live in the spirit." It is natural, therefore, and you will forgive me, that I should thus recall here that Matthew Arnold lectured hard by, in Boston; that he lectured upon Emerson, the most spiritual of American writers; that he knew Charles Eliot Norton, whose memory I am here to serve — the memory of a man who believed in the things of the spirit.

The things of the spirit. The founder of this Chair would have been content, I fancy, to let just that phrase stand for the range of interests which he wished to prescribe to the holder of the Chair. It is to a very high demand, accordingly, that the critic of poetry must answer. And not the critic of poetry merely, but, let me add at once, the student of it. We live, I fear, too much with subterfuge; we do not always face our own high phrases quite honestly. In our best study of poetry, and not merely in our casual comments upon it, are we always, or often, sensible that the criticism of poetry is the study of things spiritual? And in what sense is it so?

The great men whom I have named brought to the subject a strong degree of moral prepossession. To-

day, just that moral prepossession is, to a good many
persons, alienating; and to not a few positively ter-
rifying. We live, I suppose, in an age of frayed
nerves: I cannot explain otherwise what I observe in
perhaps one half the students of poetry whom I meet,
their nervous apprehension of a poetry which is going
to make them better. They run from a poetry which
promises to improve them with an indecent hurry
hardly to be excused if it threatened their complete
moral corruption. What the origins are of this strong
anti-ethical prejudice, I do not know. But they are
more recent than we like to believe — I sometimes
wonder whether they can be traced much beyond the
period of the French decadents.

Traced, I mean, in the student of poetry, as distinguished from the theorist of it: I leave out of account,
that is, the labours of the philosophers and aestheticians, all the long history of the metaphysic of art.
There have never in any age been wanting philosophers to tell the poet his business. If poets have not
yet discovered, or have discovered only recently, that
poetry and virtue have nothing to do with one an-
o her, it is not the fault of the professors of aesthetic.
Yet their speculations have, in fact, been curiously
inoperative. Of the immense body of aesthetic theory
which exists in the world, three fifths is, I should suppose, German, and almost nothing of it has carried to
the poets and men of letters. For this inoperativeness
of aesthetic theory it is not easy to assign reasons.
Too much, it may be, of what has been written upon
the theory of art has been written by persons, I will

not say insensitive to the great examples of the practice of it, but sensitive with a sensitiveness too closely
guarded. Or is it merely that aesthetic theory is *hard*,
and that, do what you may, you will never persuade
either the man in the street, or the poet in his solitude,
that the beautiful is hard — that it is anything but
divinely easy?

I will not pretend to say. Nor will I ask what the
causes are of the anti-ethical fashion which at the present governs so powerfully both the study and the
practice of poetry. For so I think it is; the flight from
ethics may be seen all along the line — at some
points of the line it is conducted in a temper almost
disorderly. Nor is it anywhere, perhaps, exempt
from what is incident to all flight, some element of the
ludicrous. I am interested here, however, merely to
notice how modern this anti-ethical prepossession
really is. It would have shocked an intelligent Greek.
It would have seemed nonsense to any serious Roman; who would have asked, with that naïve practicality which makes the Romans so impressive,
"What, then, is poetry for?" Upon his faith in the
power of poetry to humanise, to moralise, to mould
character, to inspire action, the Roman built his
whole system of education. Education was practi-
cally synonymous with the study of the poets. The
poets made a man brave, the poets made a man eloquent, the poets made him — if anything could make
him — poetical. "The poet," says Horace, "fashions
the child's unformed and lisping speech, and early
wrests his ear from all gross discourse. Anon, with

rules of life which commend themselves of their own
sweetness, he moulds his heart, correcting in him all
ungentle thoughts, and envy and anger. He recounts
to him deeds nobly done, and with great examples
arrays his dawn of youth." It is no longer the fashion,
I know, to place Horace among the great poets of the
world. Yet which of them, I sometimes wonder, has
influenced more profoundly the thought and feeling
of the centuries? I am at least so far with Horace that
I think it hard to overestimate the obscure benefit to
the national life of a discipline in which the thought
and language of the best poetry are the earliest form-
ative influences.

The moral prepossession which dominated antiquity communicated itself to the Renaissance — the
Italian Renaissance, the French Renaissance, our
own Renaissance. In that new birth of the human
imagination men still continued so simple in their
thinking that hardly one of them but supposed that,
for the purpose of making men better, the most
powerful of instruments was poetry. In that spirit
and faith Sidney wrote; in that spirit and faith Ben
Jonson; in that faith, held even with some touch of
fanaticism, Milton. If the temper of the men of the
eighteenth century was different, was more worldly,
yet they too thought of poetry as having, for its most
important function, the power to refine life, to give
virtue and manners. And the tradition passes to the
great romantics. The obvious names I leave aside.
But we do not look, perhaps, to find Byron among the
moralists. Yet what does he say? "The highest of all

poetry," he writes, "is the ethical, as the highest of all objects must be moral truth." The trouble is, indeed, not to find witnesses — the cloud of them is overpowering — but to discover somewhere a great poet, a great man of letters, who does not bind up his art with that of virtue. That it is not the business of a great writer to teach virtue is in fact an almost absurdly modern thesis. So much so that, when Matthew Arnold said that poetry was "a criticism of life," "mainly on the side of morality," — really, I do not suppose that he stopped to think. Who of such writers as he was likely to study — unless it were Goethe — had ever said anything else? He gave paradoxical finish, and a too-sharp expression, to what, for five-and-twenty centuries, had passed for a truism with poets and men of letters. He was unlucky in that he dropped his truism among just those conditions in which it was likely to be exploded in laughter: the conditions of the French decadence, and the movements aping it.

At the risk of being thought to have died somewhere about the year in which I was born, I will say frankly that I find it difficult to attach no value at all to the persistent belief of poets that it is their office to make men better; that, whether or not they aim to do it, to do it belongs to their office or effect. I find it difficult, again, to dismiss as mere illusion the sense which so many of us have, when we read poetry, that it is good for us, that we are the better for it. When I am told that it is the business of poetry to make me, not better, but more poetical, I have the sense that I am being entertained with a distinction unnecessarily fine. Poetical values are, after all, values in a human life. You cannot mark them off from other human values, as though the nature of man were built in bulkheads: as though there were a department of poetry hermetically sealed, a kind of padded room of aesthetic so effectively sound-proof that the ravings of poesy are unable to disturb either the moral sense in us or the instinct for truth.

The critics who have laboured so hard to divorce poetry from morality, or at any rate to bring about a judicial separation between them, have acted primarily, I suppose, in the interest of poetry. To the forlorn situation of morality have they paid, perhaps, too little account? Poetry, they have told themselves — and it may be true — can get on very well without morality; poetry has no need of moral ideas. Do they mean, and are they equally sure, that morality can do without poetry? Has morality no need of that quickening of vital forces which poetry gives? Morality, no one I suppose will deny, is one of the great interests of mankind. Yet most of us, I should fancy, feel that, with no other inspiration than that furnished by the facts of life, by prose, it is a dull, a hard, an unlovely business — for myself, I should be ready to call it an impossible business. The condition of morality, I would suggest, is the more gloomy in that its alienation from poetry has coincided in time with that shaking of religious beliefs, that criticism of all creeds, which makes the latter half of the nineteenth century so momentous an era. "There is not a creed which is not shaken," wrote Matthew Arnold in 1880, "not an accredited dogma which is not shown to be questionable, not a received tradition which does not threaten to dissolve." "Most of what now passes," he adds, "most of what now passes with us for religion and philosophy will be replaced by poetry." You see what he is after. Religion, so long wedded to morality, is dead; Matthew Arnold is projecting for the widow a new married happiness with poetry. Alas, he little knew poetry, of which the genius is so severely dedicated to self-expression as to have given to her character a permanent cast of incompatibility. She was married once to music; but she broke away. We had supposed her not long since securely wedded to verse; she has shaken herself free. That she should take the leavings of religion, that she should live with moral ideas — to think that was to think in a fashion patently academic.

That poetry is very well able, now and at all times, to look after itself; that poetry is, like morality, one of those vital human interests which are never seriously imperilled; that whatever false direction it may from time to time take, in the long run it may be trusted to right itself: this no one doubts who brings any effort of genuine study either to poetry or to human nature. But that poetry always becomes better, that it moves always in a true and straight line of advance, this the whole history of poetry plainly refutes. That period of our poetry, for example, which lies between the death of Milton and the birth of Wordsworth has its demonstrable excellences, which I have no wish to

decry. Yet think of what preceded; and what a fall
from power that whole century is!

Of the poetry which immediately preceded poetry
as we know it today, I have never been the undiscrim-
inating champion. It had those faults which made
the present reactions from it inevitable. But when
you have catalogued its faults, at least you must
allow to it that it was animated by a certain greatness
of mind. I had the good fortune to light the other day
upon some observations by a living poetess, Miss
Sackville West, upon *Tendencies of Modern English
Poetry*. Of the poetry of the twentieth century Miss
Sackville West knows more than I can ever hope to
do; and of her many interesting observations upon it
one impressed me especially. "It is impossible," she
writes, "to imagine, even after allowing for changes
of diction, a Gray's 'Elegy,' or an 'Ode on (the) Intimations of Immortality,' still less a 'Prelude,' or a
'Paradise Lost,' as the product of the twentieth century. . . . I do not believe that even a great poet,
were one to arise, could or would move upon the plane
or breathe the air of Milton and Wordsworth. This is
simply another way of saying that sublimity has gone
out of fashion."

I do not know that I much like, in its context, the
word "sublimity": it carries associations which do
not sort, I think, with Gray's *Elegy*, nor with the
Prelude of Wordsworth, nor even, perhaps, with the
"Immortal Ode." But I will not quarrel over a word.
The author of the ancient treatise *On the Sublime* has
called sublimity an "echo of magnificence of mind."

That quality, magnificence of mind — a quality, whatever name you choose for it, easily recognisable — that quality is, I think we must agree with Miss Sackville West, wanting in the poetry of the last thirty years, it may be of the last fifty. I do not like to say, with Miss Sackville West, that it has "gone out of fashion." Something deeper than fashion governs, surely, the shining and setting of this starry virtue. There has passed a glory from our poetry, however, of which the presence is, in the poems which Miss Sackville West names, plainly discernible, and of which we still catch the last rays in the poetry of the great Victorians. There are, of course, many idiosyncrasies of detail, new notes of speech and verse, fresh coin of curious thought, which mark the poetry of today as different from poetry as we have hitherto known and accepted it; but the deepest difference, the most pervasive, consists beyond a doubt in the defect of that quality which I call magnificence of mind.

The difference is a difference of moral plane — only so can I conceive it, and, at risk of being misunderstood, express it.

I say at risk of being misunderstood; for I know very well what I may *seem* to say. "Poetry is in a bad way; we have a sick man on our hands; and we can only treat this sickness with what Dryden calls "a crude preparation of morals." I may seem to say that; but there is nothing that I less wish to say: very heartily do I endorse Dryden when he says that "a crude preparation of morals . . . we may have from Aristotle and Epictetus with more profit than from any poet." Yet I do ask the poet to teach, I do believe him to teach: *only*, in his own fashion, and his own lessons. It is not the fashion, and they are not the lessons, of what is called didactic poetry. There is no man of us, I suppose, who does not hate didactic poetry; all the man in any one of us is in protest against it, a protest instinctive and decisive. Yet not because it teaches; far rather because it so signally fails to teach; there is nothing to be learned from it; and what we resent is its incompetence. We tell ourselves that we hate a poetry which has a design upon us; above all, when it has a moral design. We like poetry to hit the mark, but we do not like it to aim. That is to be, perhaps, over-exigent; and in truth, what we really hate, I suspect, is less a moral aim than a moral miss. I have mentioned Gray's *Elegy*. I should be inclined to call Gray's *Elegy* one of the great moral hits of literature. Like every other great poem, it can be read with sophistication, though, mostly, it has had the good luck to be read with heart. To the great commonplaces of living and dying it gives perfect classical expression. Allow to the element of expression all that you will; allow to language and rhythm their proper mystery and mastery; even so, it will require a good deal of sophistication to express the sum of this poem in terms other than those of moral power. It has lived long in men's hearts; it has been read by men who, reading it, conceived themselves to be made better, and not merely more poetical.

When Wolfe read it to his officers, he did not want them to be poetical, he wanted them to take Quebec.

Frankly, I do not know what it is that we are all so frightened of. Moral ideas are not going to bite us, that, when we meet them here, or in some other poetry, we should bury our heads in the bedclothes, seeking safety in form and expression, until the ethical terror be overpast. I sometimes wonder whether what we are afraid of is not, in fact, poetry itself. Suppose that to some intelligent enquirer from Mars or the moon, it were explained that poetry was the highest form of human speech; suppose that the same enquirer, interested in man's thousand activities, were told that the highest human interests were truth and virtue, and that these were frequent subjects of discussion among men, that men were keenly concerned to communicate and exchange with one another their experience in connexion with truth and virtue; suppose such an enquirer to ask in what speech such communication took place; what would he expect to be told? That we kept our best speech for our second-best interests? that we left it to prose to speak of truth and virtue? Our man in the moon would go back to the moon, surely, earth-struck and perplexed.

Of all the arts, let me here observe, poetry is the nearest to prose. That is a very obvious reflection; so obvious that our thinking sometimes misses it, and rarely, I fancy, attends to its implications. For is not this a very serious situation for poetry — to be so near prose, to hold its station always on the edge of that precipice, to have only this hair-breadth remove from the very negation of itself? I cannot think that poetry stands thus near to prose *for nothing*. It runs this daily danger of being prose just because it exists, not for its own sake (as perhaps some other arts do), but for ours, to serve essentially human needs. It is near to prose for the opportunities of *discourse*, for the communication of experience. It has deliberately elected to *say* things; and having made that election, is it not going to say the things that most matter? Is it likely to overlook truth and virtue? Does it not know, what all of us know, how incompetently these great interests are, in fact, handled by prose, what a death-in-life the so-called moral life is unless it be irradiated by the imagination? Is it not just this which has called poetry into being — the sheer incompetence of prose to give meaning to what should mean everything to us? Here in truth is what staggers the aestheticians — the immensity of the sacrifice made by poetry; who, when she might have been music, or some imagined ecstasy, elected to occupy a middle station, a station somewhere between prose and (may I say it?) the divine Logos. Alone of the arts she has put on humanity.

Singularly wanting in humanity would she be, however, if she were always preaching to us, always iterating moral truths; singularly wanting, moreover, in that of which she is, we know, "all compact" — imagination. Such a poem as Gray's *Elegy* cannot happen every day; the poet of it must watch for his hour. In the sense in which Gray's *Elegy* is a purely ethical composition, it is hard for poetry to be ethical. Yet look at the matter in another way, and it is hard for it not to be ethical. I say nothing of the fact that it uses ethical instruments; rhythms which have their correspondences in conditions of soul; words which have a world-old tradition in the feeling heart. But it cannot escape from its own magnificence of mind; say what it may, its accents will render always an authentic echo of that magnificence. Whatever the theme, the ideas of the imagination tend to fall with an ethical ring. The Stoics had a proverb, *Digitum exsere, peccas* — put out your little finger, and you sin. You betray character; you cannot help yourself. Well, put out the little finger of the imagination, I would say, and you express virtue. Whether you like it or not, that happens. Virtue must be conceived, of course, largely, generously, even extravagantly — some extravagance of direction is, indeed, in the very nature of it.

The ideas of the imagination fall with an ethical ring. We tend sometimes to speak of poetry as though it were directed, not from human beings to human beings, but proceeded from a kind of men in the moon towards some other men in the moon. Certainly I have no wish to challenge its etherial quality. But those who disclaim for poetry all taint of the teaching office, yet commonly allow, I think, that it endeavours to be, that it has a duty to be, interesting: indeed, that seems dictated to it by a law of self-preservation. But interesting to whom? Not to a world, surely, of men in the moon, but to a world of human creatures: of human creatures with prepossessions, the prepossessions of their kind. Of human prepos-

sessions hardly any is stronger than the moral.
Neither can the poet escape it, for he is not born of an
oak or a rock, but of men; nor, if he could, would he
find, in a world of men, acceptance. He would be
just uninteresting. He conceives morality widely —
so widely that sometimes another name seems wanted
for it; — and not merely widely, but deeply — in
that depth which can hold nature's obscurest peccan-
cies. But he cannot escape it. It is interesting to
watch here and there a poet struggling against the
very consequences of himself, fighting the ethical bias
as though it were some deadly propensity; to see with
what fine spirit he carries the unequal strife, to see
him, nonetheless, perpetually caught back into the
whirlpool of nature, a moralist *malgré lui*. And after
all, what is he fighting for? Freedom, freedom of the
spirit: a moral cause. More often than not, I fancy,
he has misconceived the nature of freedom; he has
thought of it as something negative, the absence of
restraints, and not as a positive ideal, the realisation
of powers, the full sense of human energies.

Do all the poets, then, teach virtue, and is that
what I mean to say? Well, if we may believe Protag-
oras, the teachers of virtue are the whole of society.
I am inclined to think that he was right. All of us
teach virtue. But some of us do it better than others.
The poet does it better than anyone else, and more
insistently, partly because he uses instruments of art
(a special language and an idiom of rhythm) which
are (for whatever reason) more subtle and effective
than any others; and partly, we must believe, because

his nature is more intensely engaged for the cause of life, for the well-being of man in its widest conception. He has a finer ear for, a heart more open to, the remotest murmur of our human needs. He brings to the hidden issues of life those gifts of passionate perception which belong to a nature moving habitually on the plane of magnificence of mind. Out of that magnificence of mind with which he lives he irradiates all themes; in such a way that often it seems hardly to matter on what subject he speaks. The least and lightest part of his utterance falls, if I may not say with a moral ring, yet with the ring of some essential rightness of nature. Yet the subject is not indifferent to him, as I think; but in proportion as he has magnificence of mind he is drawn to great themes. That all themes are, in poetry, equally good, that the thesis of any art is indifferent, I have never been brought to persuade myself. It is the fashion to believe it, a fashion which has not wanted, I know, metaphysical backing. Even so, when I am told that a great action and a good dinner are themes equally acceptable to, and in, poetry; or when, to take a concrete example, I am asked to believe that Homer's account of the wrath of Achilles and Herrick's account of Julia's dress ("Whenas in silks my Julia goes") are, if poetry, equally poetry — always, not merely my reason, but what I value almost as much, all the cheerful Philistinism in me, revolts. Nor can I be placated by being told that, while these two themes are equally poetry, the one is in fact more valuable for its added moral content. There *is* no added content; for precisely in the inseparable conjunction of the content and the form lies the poetry.

I cannot but think that in recent years both poetry and the criticism of poetry have fallen upon sophistication. It is perhaps natural to youth to be sophistical — it can afford it. I wish that I knew the poetry of the twentieth century better than I do. That is only to wish myself younger than I am; for I cannot know it by reading in it, but only by being in it and of it. So far as I know it, I find in it so many qualities which I value — chief among them, its astonishing fecundity of technical power, but on the side of spirit also, its questing energy, its fierce curiosity — I find in it so many qualities which I value that it is perhaps ungenerous in me to sum its effects by saying, what I yet feel to be true, that it has every gift but wants magnificence of mind. I would not say that if it had not been said for me already by a well-accredited witness, by the accomplished poetess whom I quoted just now, who conceives this quality as having "gone out of fashion." I deprecated the phrase. But the fall from fashion of this quality, its loss, its temporary obscuration — call it what you will — is hardly unconnected, I feel, with the dominance in poetry of that theory of it which supposes it to exist for its own sake and to die at the breath of moral ideas. Of a poetry which exists for its own sake, the real danger is that it will die, not of moral ideas, but of being uninteresting. Necessarily, it disconnects itself from the great interests of life. It can support a lingering existence by being interesting in a variety of temporary modes, by starts of novelty, by effects of the bizarre or perverse. These are but the shifts and paltering of sophistry. Sooner or later poetry, poetry destined to live, to live and to communicate life, must make return upon the source of life, must come home to magnificence of mind.

❖❖❖❖❖❖❖❖❖❖❖❖❖❖❖❖❖❖❖❖❖❖

THE POETRY OF
MATTHEW ARNOLD

I

I CANNOT believe that I need any excuse for speaking of Matthew Arnold in Harvard: for giving him a first place: for giving him two first places — devoting to him, I mean, a double lecture.[1] He has many demands on my piety: the nature of some of them I indicated sufficiently, I may suppose, last week, when, speaking here for the first time, I took as my subject a thesis with which his name is very specially associated. Upon my own piety he has many demands; and some — may I suggest? — upon yours. When he came to Cambridge in 1883 — he was the guest here of Charles Eliot Norton — he came, he said, to a neighbourhood of which the names were "invested to *his* ear with a sentiment akin to that which invest*ed* for *him* the names of Oxford and of Weimar." In Oxford, he had listened to the preaching of Newman; in Oxford, or the tradition of Oxford, he had lived his highest life:

> There where the spirit its highest life hath lived,
> All spots, matched with that spot, are less divine.

Goethe he rated as "Europe's sagest head," and the little town of Weimar — "wie Bethlehem in Juda,

---

[1] I had intended to lecture on Matthew Arnold only as a poet. The lecture *Matthew Arnold as Critic* was added later.

klein und gross" — as one of the world's great
shrines, an oracular seat. Yet another seat of oracles,
oracles perhaps of less certain tone, yet of the genuine
Pythian tradition, was what he calls "Emerson's
country." "At last I find myself in Emerson's own
country," he says: like one who has found a long-
sought spiritual contentment. We may forgive him if
he uses the occasion to moralise upon a common and
perhaps saddening experience. How' few of the literary idols of our youth, he exclaims, support the return
upon them of our mature judgment! "But we must
make the return, we must part with our illusions."

I suppose we must. Even so, it is one thing to part
with our illusions, and another thing, a harder thing,
indeed a thing impossible, to part with having had
them. Our good deeds, says George Eliot, senten-
tiously, and a little prosaically,

> Our good deeds travel with us from afar,
> And what we have been makes us what we are.

Well, our good reading, and our bad reading, travel
with us, similarly. I am sometimes frightened when I
reflect upon the bare accidents that conduct us to our
first books, the first books, I mean, which give a real
direction to our lives. For the most part, I suppose,
we read the books that are being read; the last
written, that means — as often as not. That is why
there is no such good fortune as to live in an age in
which good literature is being created. A fortune
which you will esteem good or bad according to your
prejudices threw my youth upon the last decades of

that variously judged era, the Victorian. I think I
never much liked it; and if I did not, I owed it to
Matthew Arnold. What chance first brought me to
him, I well remember; though it was, indeed, not
chance, but wise direction. I came to him first by
way of his Introduction to Wordsworth; and I was
put upon that, in a fashion prosaical enough, by one
of my schoolmasters. I say "prosaical," but, in
truth, it was nothing of the kind. Perhaps I was
fifteen; but I remember the day, not merely well, but
with vivid exactness, and the very expressions in
which the book was commended to me. Before that,
I was interested in poetry; I have the suspicion that I
both read and wrote it. But this was my first introduction to literary criticism, on that level, at least, on
which it is itself literature; and it was my first en-
counter with distinction in prose style. From the
essay on Wordsworth I passed, I believe, to the Lectures on Homer. How fresh and great they were, how
loftily they conceived poetry how they put me out of
love, I remember, with the poetry of Tennyson! I
was to be put out of love, later, with Shelley; or, half
out of love, for some instinct warned me here that I
was being led by an idiosyncrasy of judgment, by
some false direction of a taste generally true and sure.
I was to be led to question much that I had been
used to believe, and not merely in poetry. I read
Literature and Dogma, I read *God and the Bible*; thinking much of literature, despising dogma, using the
Bible intelligently, and proud to define God as a
"stream of tendency." You need, not merely to have

lived in that period, but to have been young in it, to have been, perhaps, not merely young but clever, to realise the very special influence which the writings of Matthew Arnold then exercised over the mind of aspiring youth. How we loved "sweetness and light," with what an almost sensuous addiction! How we despised "Philistines" and "barbarians," and indeed nine tenths of our countrymen. What devotees we were, what initiates, of "the grand manner," not confining the operation of it to literature, but wherever we went carrying with us the enthusiasm of it — I fancy it was with us even if we went nowhere, making its unpopular appearance often in the domestic circle.

In saying so much, I have been thinking of that influence which Matthew Arnold exercised by his prose writings. At the time of which I speak he passed, I think without much question, for the first of English critics, our first man of letters. But the power of his poetry was much less widely felt. Common opinion, at least while he lived, hardly brought him into the rank of the great poets. The student of poetry conceded to him — perhaps grudgingly — the third place among the poets of his age, putting him decisively below both Tennyson and Browning. He was a professor of poetry first, and a poet in a degree definitely secondary. That represents fairly, I think, the judgment of him current in my youth. Unless I am mistaken, the last thirty years have reversed it; and I admire the justice of time. I am sorry that Matthew Arnold's critical writings have so much gone out of fashion; for that it is so I have no doubt. I am sensible of faults in them which, thirty years ago, I missed; there are other persons I think who are offended by their virtues. I am not sure that I should still venture to call him the greatest of the English critics; I should be disposed, I fancy, to assign a higher place to Hazlitt. Yet, while I rate his criticism highly, I rejoice to see popular judgment steadily hardening to a preference for his poetry. If that judgment expresses itself, in respect of his criticism, in terms which are, I think, unduly disparaging — as though it belonged to an outworn mode — that does not much matter, that will right itself presently.

It is perhaps worth while to remind you, in any case, that it was out of being a poet that Matthew Arnold became, in fact, a professor of poetry. The Oxford professorship was the foundation of his fame. Yet when he was elected to it, in 1857, he had written no criticism, he had no critical reputation.[1] He was elected upon the repute of his poetry, upon that and nothing else. The electors to the Chair were, as they still are, the graduate strength of the University, the whole body of Oxford Masters. Never say, therefore, that an extreme democracy lacks fine perceptions. Matthew Arnold was elected upon the repute of a poetry about which he had been, in fact, singularly shy. He had printed his first volume of verse in 1849; very few copies of it had been sold when he withdrew it from the press. He published a second volume in

[1] The 1853 volume of his Poems, however, was introduced by a Preface, subsequently relegated to his prose works, in which for the first time he voices, upon poetry generally and upon particular errancies of modern taste, opinions which his later criticism amplifies infinitely.

1852; and again, not fifty copies were in circulation before he stopped the issue. Both volumes were published under a pseudonym (if the initial "A" may be so called) and today they are bibliographical rarities. Most of the pieces in them, with the exception of *Empedocles on Etna*, Matthew Arnold reprinted either in 1853 or in 1855. With those reprinted in 1853 he printed also, for the first time, *Sohrab and Rustum*, as well as *The Scholar Gipsy* and the famous *Requiescat* ("Strew on her roses, roses . . ."). The 1855 volume contained also a new poem, *Balder Dead*.

It was upon this record that Matthew Arnold was elected in 1857 to the Chair which was to be for ten years his critical pulpit. His accession to the Chair he inaugurated by the publication of *Merope*, his leaving of it, in 1867, by a volume entitled *New Poems*, a somewhat delusive title, for nearly all that was worth having had been either composed or published many years before.

From having been a poet, then, Matthew Arnold became a professor; and from being a professor, many people will tell you, he ceased to be a poet. It would not surprise me, if it were true; I take it to be, in fact, a little short of the truth. The date at which Matthew Arnold ceased to be effectively a poet must be put earlier: you must go back to 1853; between 1853 and 1857 his only work in poetry is *Balder Dead*.

Of his first two volumes Arthur Hugh Clough wrote, here in Cambridge, for the *North American Review*, a not too sympathetic criticism. In the same notice he included the Poems of Alexander Smith. Of

Alexander Smith, Matthew Arnold was always a little impatient — it was not jealousy; like a good many men who have a just sense of their own merits, he was jealous of nobody. Smith was a Glasgow mechanic, Matthew Arnold, what Clough calls him, apologetically, "a scholar and a gentleman." Clough's sympathies, nowhere openly avowed, are pretty obviously with the humbler station and the inferior poet. About Matthew Arnold's poetry he lived, as one of Arnold's letters remarks, in a permanent state of suspended judgment. This was the period, moreover, of what Arnold called "Citizen Clough." "Citizen Clough" had come to America in search of higher values than those which connect with the typically English fetish of the scholar and the gentleman. His temper was a good deal more robust than that of Matthew Arnold. We forget that, commonly; because we remember him best as Matthew Arnold has delivered him to us, we remember him by *Thyrsis*:

> It irked him to be here, he could not rest,
> For that a shadow loured on the fields.

It was the shadow of the scholar and the gentleman, though it does not suit Matthew Arnold to say so. I suspect, moreover, that Clough was a good deal more robust in Cambridge than he was at home and in Oxford (I understand that). Accordingly, not merely in the poetry of Matthew Arnold, but in the literature of Europe generally, he discovers "a disposition to press too far the finer and subtler intellectual and moral susceptibilities." Europe can be left to look after itself (as America has taught us). But the disposition that Clough here arraigns, the "disposition to press too far the finer and subtler intellectual and moral susceptibilities," the disposition which may be expressed, perhaps, — not too finely nor too subtly — as a kind of spiritual *fussiness*; this disposition is present, it does manifest itself, in the poetry of Matthew Arnold. It was a stroke of criticism merely to juxtapose Arnold and the Glasgow mechanic. I recall a remark about fellows of colleges made somewhere by Walter Raleigh, himself a fellow of a college. The exact phrasing of it I forget; but "fellows of colleges" he says, in effect, "are only truly judged when brought into comparison with Glasgow mechanics" — it is some other trade that he names, brewers' draymen, I fancy; but it makes no difference. It is a hard saying, but ponderable, and with enough of plausibility to make one uneasy. At least it is a good thing to look off sometimes from our poetry, and from our criticism, to the plainer tasks of the drayman or the mechanic.

I will not deny, what I think Clough believed, that the poetry of Matthew Arnold would be the better for some stiffening from the temper of either of those trades. Even so, I tire a little of Clough's practicality, his insistence on action:

> And not for colouring idle dust,
>   And not for piping empty reeds —
> If live we positively must,
>   God's name be praised for noble deeds.

That is spirited enough. But, like Matthew Arnold, Clough had the preaching habit; and "Get on with

your job: the soul is not as fine as all that," that is a
too favourite text with him. If I did not hate "Dia-
logues of the Dead," I should like to make a dialogue
of Clough and Matthew Arnold; and I would see to it
that Matthew Arnold had the better of it. "You may
be right," he should say to Clough; "the soul is not as
fine as all that. But it *is* ever so fine; too fine for the
coarse finger and thumb of the world. And as for
brewers' draymen and mechanics — one of Her Majesty's Inspectors of Schools, why, what a brewer's
drayman am I, and what a *plusquam* mechanic, since
I do not operate a machine, but am in fact operated
by one. And withal, I have undertaken to keep alive
the soul in me!"

The sense how difficult it is to keep alive the soul
broods over, and informs, the whole of Matthew
Arnold's poetry. Somewhere — I think in the essay
upon Wordsworth — he speaks in a tone rather
slighting of Wordsworth's great Ode — the Ode, I
mean, on Intimations of Immortality. Not only does
he find in it — if I remember rightly — some element
of the declamatory, but he expresses himself scepti-
cally, or uneasily, about its truth of substance. I
have never very well understood that; or if I have, I
have understood very ill, not some one part, but all
parts, of Matthew Arnold's poetry.

> Ah! not the nectarous poppy lovers use,
> Not daily labour's dull Lethaean spring,
> Oblivion in lost angels can infuse
> Of the soiled glory and the trailing wing.

That is from a poem of his first volume of poems; and
the source of inspiration is obvious:

> Our birth is but a sleep and a forgetting,
> The soul that rises with us, our life's star,
> Hath had elsewhere its setting,
> And cometh from afar.
> Not in entire forgetfulness,
> And not in utter nakedness,
> But trailing clouds of glory do we come
> From God, who is our home.

"The soul that rises with us, our life's star." Go now,
from Matthew Arnold's first volume, to his last; and
take from it these lines, of which Clough would have
liked, I fancy, the virile note, their accent of perhaps
rather weary courage:

> Still doth the soul from its lone fastness high,
> Upon our life a ruling effluence send;
> And when that fails, fight as we will, we die,
> And while it lasts, we cannot wholly end.

Matthew Arnold took for true, what I think Wordsworth took for true, what we are happy if we do not
find, each of us, growing older, to be true in our own
experience, that the hardest thing in the world is to
keep alive the poetry in us. The "vision splendid"
which the soul has had "in some other place," the
radiance which still lights our first thinking, our earliest imaginative motions, which still attends that
youth in us which "daily further from the east Must
travel," this visionary faculty, the instinctive perception of the beauty of the world, grows less as we move
further into life:

> At length the man perceives it die away
> And fade into the light of common day.

None the less, there *is* "something that doth live," of which the "immortal Ode" makes as much as possible, converting its elegiac strains, indeed, into a paean of joy:

> O joy! that in our embers
> Is something that doth live!

But in what after all does it consist? Its sources of power Wordsworth catalogues in terms sufficiently general. Obstinate questionings, fallings from us, vanishings, dismays; mysterious instincts, shaking us with a sense as of guilt, shadowy recollections, and first loves that still are last — it is the glow of these nothings in the embers of our worldly life that attests the tenuous life of the soul.

How impermanent the conditions are of imaginative vision, Wordsworth's own poetry furnishes the practical demonstration — the best power of it is crowded into a ten-years period, hardly outliving the date at which the great Ode was finished. Thereafter, those "seasons of calm weather," of which the Ode speaks, in which the soul has sight of the immortal seas, become rare and ever rarer.

I do not know how much of Matthew Arnold's poetry does not say again what Wordsworth had said in the Ode: repeating Wordsworth's disquietudes; reaffirming, but with far from equal confidence, his grounds of consolation. There is "something that doth live"; but even so it is nothing to shout a paean over. How slender the life of it is, Matthew Arnold's poetry demonstrates in a fashion even more practical than that of Wordsworth. So brief is his poetic course that it is hardly begun in 1849, and may almost be said to conclude itself with the publication in 1853 of *Sohrab and Rustum* and *The Scholar Gipsy*. Thereafter, it is true, his artistic control is sufficiently sure to make anything that he may write interesting, to give it worth and dignity. *Balder Dead* has worth and dignity; so has *Merope*. Yet fix attention upon *Sohrab and Rustum* and *The Scholar Gipsy*: after them what is there which is of equal quality with them? Except for *Thyrsis*, I think you would find it hard to name more than, it may be, three pieces.

Matthew Arnold begins to be a poet in the volume of 1849. Of that book the best successes are *Mycerinus* and the lines *To A Gipsy Child*; both nobly classical compositions. It contains also one or two good sonnets; sonnets (as we might expect) of the severest form, Petrarchian in pattern. It ends with *Resignation*, a poem which has many beauties, but which has won for itself, I cannot but think, a higher place in the affections of Matthew Arnold's admirers than it can justly claim. Frankly, when I study it, I do not very well know what it is set to say; I find no real development in its reflection. In particular, I have never been able to divine what the difference is which is supposed to divide the poet and Fausta. About Fausta, I confess to a perhaps trivial curiosity. *Resignation* brings her into the region of the English Lakes — she was, I suspect, not native there — and commemorates a ten-years friendship with Matthew Arnold, carrying us back, therefore, to 1839, when he was a youth of eighteen. To Fausta is addressed also the poem entitled *The Question*. Nothing hints that the poet's relation to her was stretched beyond the terms of friendship. But she is his confidante; an interesting and responsible position. Side by side with *The Question* stood, in 1849, *The Voice*; and upon the circumstances lying behind that poem, I should like to have been able to interrogate Fausta. *The Voice* is not hers; it is the voice, it is difficult to doubt, of a person a good deal more interesting, upon whose identity our guesses are still spent in vain: it can hardly be any other voice than that of Marguerite:

> So sad, and with so wild a start,
> To this deep-sobered heart. . .
>
> And oh, with such intolerable change
> Of thought, such contrast strange,
> O unforgotten voice, thy accents come,
> Like wanderers from the world's extremity,
>   Unto their ancient home!
>
> In vain, all, all in vain,
> They beat upon my ear again,
> Those melancholy tones so sweet and still,
> Those lute-like tones which in the bygone year
> Did steal into my ear —
> Blew such a thrilling summons to my will,
> Yet could not shake it;
> Made my lost heart its very life-blood spill,
>   Yet could not break it.

Marguerite is almost as intriguing as Wordsworth's Lucy. Except for *The Voice* (which does not name her), she is represented in the volume of 1849 only by the poem entitled *A Memory Picture*, a piece lightly, almost gaily, conceived, and, no doubt, early; by that, and perhaps more significantly by the fact that she has lent her name to the lost bride of *The Forsaken Merman*. That poem, once again, though it has always been a favourite with students of Matthew Arnold — it was one of Clough's favourites — I sometimes think to be, like *Resignation*, a little overrated. The hour of Marguerite, in any case, was not yet come. Or rather, it had not yet gone by; it was not yet enough past to submit to that transmuting power which converts what we suffer into the song that redeems us out of suffering. For that, we have to wait for the volume of 1852, the volume which Matthew Arnold christened, from the first poem in it, *Empedocles on Etna*.

It might better have been called *The Forsaken Merman*, and have taken into itself, from the 1849 volume, both the poem of that title and *The Voice*. For it is Marguerite's book, the book of forsaken or separated lovers; how much it is so I do not know that we always sufficiently realise. The central portion of the book is occupied by *Tristram and Iseult*. The case of Tristram and Iseult is that of Marguerite and her lover —

A god, a god, their severance ruled!

For Marguerite, or to meet some of the imaginings which she fired, Matthew Arnold — can we doubt it? — wrote this story; of which the form itself, mingling the romantic and the classical manners, is an interesting and significant experiment.

Fear me not, I will be always with thee,
  I will watch thee, tend thee, soothe thy pain,
Tell thee tales of true long-parted lovers
Joined at evening of their days again.

That we should not miss the significance of this tale of parted lovers, Matthew Arnold placed before it, in the volume of 1852, some of the best known pieces of the Marguerite series. I say, some of them; for the truth is that he could never bring himself to play quite fair about Marguerite. For one of the Marguerite poems, if not for three, you have to go back, I have said, to the 1849 volume. Five other poems [1] of the series Matthew Arnold released at various dates between 1853 and 1867. Even when he had parted with all the Marguerite poems, he still indulged mystification; separating from the rest the five called *Faded Leaves*, as though they had nothing to do with Marguerite — who was, indeed, by a lucky chance, not actually named in any of them. Of another poem, called originally *Indifference*, he changed the title, so that Marguerite might pass for a Greek divinity. [2] The piece called, in the final edition of his poems, *Youth and Calm*, was called, in 1852, *Lines Written by a Deathbed*. It was a woman's deathbed; though you

[1] The poem *Isolation* he kept back till 1853; yet another, similarly entitled, till 1857. *The Dream* he released in 1853. The poem called *Separation* he first printed in 1855. In the same year he published *The Terrace at Berne*, an epilogue to the whole series, written in 1857–59.

[2] About the poem called, in later editions, *Urania*, but in 1852 *Excuse*, I feel doubtful. The third stanza of it seems not to suit very well an earthly goddess. I suspect that, before it was printed, it had been retouched. On the whole, I think this Muse *was* Marguerite — on any other shewing the place which this poem, and *Indifference*, occupy in the volume of 1852 is inexplicable.

would never guess it from the later editions, where its first sixteen lines are missing:

Yes, now the longing is o'erpast
Which, dogg'd by fear and fought by shame,
Shook her weak bosom day and night,
Consum'd her beauty like a flame
And dimm'd it like the desert blast. . . .

So it begins, or began. Who is this woman, in whose bosom longing contended with shame and fear, consuming her beauty like a fire? Did Matthew Arnold indulge, in respect of Marguerite, the morbid habit which Coleridge supposes Wordsworth to have indulged in respect of his sister — did he figure her dead, and write her epitaph? To what order of world, in any case, did Marguerite belong? *The Terrace at Berne* speaks of her as one whose feet came too lightly down the flowery track; and in the same poem her lover wonders whether she is one of those persons who, when they reach years of indiscretion, become rouged and riotous.

I am sorry to say it, but I am afraid that Matthew Arnold lived to be a little ashamed of Marguerite. When he made his final arrangement of his poems, he was willing that she should appear in his poetry as a diversion; he did not wish that she should look like an obsession, even an obsession of youth. His shifts defeat themselves, emphasising what they endeavour to slur. I used at one time to pooh-pooh Marguerite. In part, I was fearful of vulgarising a great poet. In part, I did not sufficiently believe that poets mean what they say; but they do — even when they do not say what they mean; from our failure to recognise that proceed nearly all the faults of our criticism. Moreover, I had not learned to read Matthew Arnold's poems in their proper connexions: — I had a robust distaste for bibliography. I say it with hesitation, but I think now that it is a mistake to disparage Marguerite. The volume of 1852 has a somewhat surprising unity, the unity, I feel, of a single and intense experience. When you have added to it the poems which should never have been taken away, it is difficult not to assign to Marguerite an important place in that experience. I think I find her even in unlikely contexts. In such a poem as *The Buried Life*, though it does not name her, I am plainly entitled to find her; for it is confessedly a love-poem. Parts of it want poetry; and the love-interest becomes lost in a philosophy, or mythology, curiously compounded of Wordsworth and Obermann; so that I wonder what Marguerite made of it all. But it is interesting as linking up the Marguerite poems with those poems of the 1852 volume which are least like them, with those which bear most the stamp of the scholar or the philosopher. The stanzas, for example, in memory of Obermann are not about Marguerite. Yet I cannot but feel that they are *around* her:

> Farewell! Under the sky we part,
>   In this stern Alpine dell.
> O unstrung will! O broken heart!
>   A last, a last farewell!

I suppose *that* is said to Obermann; and his, I suppose, and not the poet's, is the "unstrung will" and "broken heart." But I am three parts doubtful; and, in any case, Obermann draws to him the will and heart that are like his own.

If Obermann is far from Marguerite, so too, I might suppose, is Wordsworth. Yet over two of the three poems which, in the 1852 volume, commemorate Wordsworth's death, her shadow falls plain. Take first the poem entitled *The Youth of Nature*. Before you read it, read the first of all the Marguerite poems, the lines called *A Memory Picture*:

> Take that lilac kerchief, bound
> Her soft face, her hair around;
> Tied under the archest chin
> Mockery ever ambushed in.
> Let the fluttering fringes streak
> All her pale, sweet rounded cheek.
> Ere the parting hour go by,
> Quick, thy tablets, Memory!

Read with that, perhaps, the verses in *Separation* which figure a time when "the loved form and the deep-cherished feature," the image of Marguerite in her prime, shall have faded from the soul of her poet. And then, with those lines, take these:

> Can thy pencil, O artist, restore
> The figure, the bloom of thy love,
> As she was in her morning of spring?
> Canst thou paint the ineffable smile
> Of her eyes as they rested on thine,
> Can the image of life have the glow,
> The motion of life itself?

Or take the whole, or any part, of *The Youth of Man*. The poem is a sequel to the piece preceding. But it forgets Wordsworth altogether, or it only so far re-

members him as to present before Nature two lovers,
once confident in their human strength, who feel now
the need of those consolations which only Nature can
supply:

> They gaze, and the evening wind
> Plays on their faces; they gaze —
> Airs from the Eden of youth
> Awake and stir in their soul. . . .
>
> Hush, for tears
> Begin to steal to their eyes! . . .
> Hush, for fruit
> Grows from such sorrow as theirs!
>
> And they remember,
> With piercing, untold anguish,
> The proud boasting of their youth.
> And they feel how Nature was fair.
> And the mists of delusion,
> And the scales of habit,
> Fall away from their eyes;
> And they see, for a moment,
> Stretching out, like the desert
> In its weary, unprofitable length,
> Their faded ignoble lives.

The volume of 1852 takes its title, I said, from the
first poem in it, *Empedocles on Etna*. Matthew
Arnold withdrew the poem from circulation, only re-
storing it in 1867, on the instance of Browning. Of
the first Part of it, I do not know that I should have
broken my heart if he had saved only the *Cadmus and
Harmonia* lyric. The second Part is beautiful
throughout; and the final soliloquy of Empedocles, all
that follows the words "And lie thou there, My
Laurel bough. . ." I conceive to be one of the noblest
passages in modern literature. Empedocles, so far as

he has life, has the life of his poet. Clough discovered in him something false or bogus; he seemed a man fussing about nothing. But I think he has a real enough tragedy, a tragedy very personal to his poet, and not wholly unrelated, perhaps, to the Marguerite experience. It is his tragedy to be an academic person; an academic person, not without taste and relish for "the delightful commerce of the world," but perpetually driven back from the world upon the soul; "miserably bandied to and fro" between the world and his own essential academicism:

> But mind, but thought —
> If these have been the master part of us?

Truly, that is, I think, Matthew Arnold's question. Fullness of life, says Empedocles,

> Fullness of life, and power of feeling, ye
> Are for the happy, for the souls at ease. . .

— for the souls at ease, and not for the scholars. In one of the Marguerite poems Matthew Arnold speaks of himself as bearing a heart which

> To be long loved was never framed.

The barrier between himself and Marguerite is the barrier of his own academicism.

> I blame thee not! this heart, I know
> To be long loved was never framed;
> For something in its depths doth glow
> Too strange, too restless, too untamed.
>
> And women — things that live and move
> Mined by the fever of the soul —
> They seek to find in those they love
> Stern strength, and promise of control.

They ask not kindness, gentle ways —
These they themselves have tried and known;
They ask a soul which never sways
With the blind gusts that shake their own.

I too have felt the load I bore
In a too strong emotion's sway;
I too have wished, no woman more,
This starting, feverish heart away.

I too have longed for trenchant force,
And will like a dividing spear;
Have praised the keen, unscrupulous course,
Which knows no doubt, which feels no fear. . . .

We school our manners, act our parts —
But He, who sees us through and through,
Knows that the bent of both our hearts
Was to be gentle, tranquil, true.

And though we wear out life, alas!
Distracted as a homeless wind,
In beating where we may not pass,
In seeking what we shall not find;

Yet shall we one day gain, life past,
Clear prospect o'er our being's whole;
Shall see ourselves, and learn at last
Our true affinities of soul.

We shall not then deny a course
To every thought the mass ignore;
We shall not then call hardness force,
Nor lightness wisdom any more. . .

How sweet, unreached by earthly jars,
My sister! to maintain with thee
The hush among the shining stars
The calm upon the moonlit sea!

How sweet to feel, on the boon air,
All our unquiet pulses cease!
To feel that nothing can impair
The gentleness, the thirst for peace —

The gentleness too rudely hurled
On this wild earth of hate and fear;
The thirst for peace a raving world
Would never let us satiate here.

That poem, I have sometimes fancied, expects more of Marguerite than was in her. In another poem, her lover calls her, academically, by the name of a Greek goddess, Euphrosyne — a creature too beautiful to be serious, too light to be a scholar's mistress.

I am inclined, then, to attach to the Marguerite experience an importance which, not long ago, I should have denied to it. I do not say that this experience came to Matthew Arnold in such a fashion that we can state it in the cheap terms which we best understand. Nor do I wish to narrow the experience — if anyone likes so to widen it as to see in Marguerite the symbol of a forbidden world of desire and of the senses, I will not stay to quarrel with him. *The Terrace at Berne* enables us to date approximately the period of the Marguerite influence; to place it in the years 1847–49. At least I feel that in those years may very well be sought the crisis of spirit which gives to Matthew Arnold's poetry its special character. I cannot too much lament the shyness, the supersensitiveness, which caused him to direct that there should be no life of him written; and which caused himself, or someone acting for him, to destroy, or withhold, all his early letters. I will not say that his letters begin where his poetry ends. But at least of the conditions in which it had its birth they afford no barest hint.

Save for his poems, we should not so much as know that he had ever been out of England before the year 1857; [1] and it is a real misfortune for criticism that he should be shut altogether from our observation in the critical years 1847–49. [2] From whatever experience those years furnished to him, he came back that poet which we find him. Not such a poet as his season of life should reasonably afford — he was twenty-seven — but he came back a poet asking of life, no longer joy, but peace, looking for his best consolations to Nature, watching over the life of his soul as though the least breath of action might, any moment, quench it, nursing the dwindling faculty of vision, lest "the world have dominion over him" and the poet perish undelivered. As he was when he came home, the volume of 1852 delivers him. It speaks to us of frustrated desires, of lovers whose severance was ruled by a god in the beginning of time; only of that, or of what it is perverse not to connect with it, disillusion and renunciation. The volume of 1852 was followed in the next year by *Sohrab and Rustum*. That year marks Matthew Arnold's height of strength. But he was to hold the height only for an hour.

[1] It may, however, be inferred from a letter of 1857, written to his wife, that he had been with her in France at some previous date. A letter of 1854, again, refers to a week-end excursion to Belgium.

[2] A sentence in a letter addressed to him by Clough from Rome, 23 June, 1849 ("I advertised you that I hope to be in the Geneva country in August") shews that Matthew Arnold was in Switzerland at least in the August of 1849.

THE POETRY OF
MATTHEW ARNOLD

II

SOHRAB AND RUSTUM is less a poem than the fragment of one. Indeed, if it be a poem, it is the only poem in the world that begins in the middle of a sentence:

> And the first grey of morning filled the east.

It marks, for Matthew Arnold, the first grey of a new poetical morn which, in fact, never grew to any settled glory of noonday power. Yet I ought not to speak of 'the first grey'; for the lights are, if sober, singularly pure; with a rather cold purity, if you like (I do not know), yet diffusing broadly the feeling air of a reserved dawn.

The poem gives us, not a story, but an episode: of which the culminating moment is presented with a grave art consciously reminiscent of Greek tragedy. Both Sohrab and his father are such personages as, from their position and character, satisfy the most exacting tragic canons; and the death of Sohrab at the hands of his father, by a deed of mere ignorance, offers a situation of that kind which the somewhat intellectualised drama of the Greeks was specially interested to illustrate. Upon the tragic act follows the recognition of what has been done. Here was that part of a Greek drama upon which the dramatist spent always his best pains. An essential element of almost any Attic tragedy, it was the "recognition scene" which afforded to the tragedian his best opportunity of originality. In Matthew Arnold's poem the recognition is elaborated with peculiar art. The discovery of Sohrab by his father is contrived, it is true, by means of "tokens"; a tragic artifice deprecated, or half-deprecated, by Aristotle. Sohrab is finally known by the tattoo marks which he bears pricked upon his arm. This was given to Matthew Arnold in the story as he found it. Yet even this weakness, if it be one, he has ingeniously — and by that I mean, with a fine poetic instinct — converted into a special kind of strength. Rustum recognises his son by tokens. But for Sohrab's recognition of his father no tokens are used, none are required; the romantic heart of youth never asks logical proofs. In the moment when his nameless foe shouts at him Rustum's name, Sohrab *knows* that it is his father; the flash of recognition in which the knowledge comes to him is, in fact, his undoing — for a moment his eye falls, and he is exposed to Rustum's spear-thrust. The heart and eye of Rustum are old and sceptical, *he* requires proofs; and the two characters stand here delicately contrasted. Yet even Rustum, we are made to feel, though he asks tokens, does not really want them. All the while all the flesh in him had been crying out "O boy, thy father!"

The tragic manner, studied out of Sophocles in especial, is diversified by beauties fetched from epic tradition; beauties surely Virgilian rather than

Homeric, though they are meant, I fancy, to recall Homer. Some of them, indeed, in their diffuse and soft and rather modern manner seem to belong less to epic than to epic idyll, to that species known to the Alexandrians as the *epyllion*. I am thinking in particular of what are sometimes called the long-tailed similes. Some critics find in *Sohrab* too much of this ornament. But gentler spirits (among whom I would wish to be) may be forgiven if they tire less easily of beautiful images, and are not disposed to fret too much over what element they may contain of the irrelevant and adventitious:

> And he saw that youth,
> Of age and looks to be his own dear son,
> Piteous and lovely, lying on the sand,
> Like some rich hyacinth which by the scythe
> Of an unskilful gardener has been cut,
> Mowing the garden grass-plots near its bed,
> And lies, a fragrant tower of purple bloom,
> On the mown, dying grass — so Sohrab lay,
> Lovely in death, upon the common sand . . .

The simile, there, of the hyacinth is, I suppose, in some form or other, world-old. Old too may be, for all I know, the simile of the violets, with whose "soiled tissue" is likened the wound in Sohrab's side:

> Like the soiled tissue of white violets
> Left, freshly gathered, on their native bank,
> By children whom their nurses call with haste
> Indoors from the sun's eye . . .

— yet the children called indoors by their nurses bring something that I .do not recollect from elsewhere. It is a serious thing for a poet to try to be like Homer; a still more serious thing to try to improve upon him. Out of both adventures Matthew Arnold comes off, I fancy, more than once with credit:

> And now all strength was ebbed, and from his limbs
> Unwillingly the spirit fled away,
> Regretting the warm mansion that it left,
> And youth, and bloom, and this delightful world.

There are four lines that recall, as they were meant to do, two famous lines of Homer. They have an air more soft and modern than Homer's lines, the rhythm dropping to the languorous; and there will be severe scholars who will like them less on that account; and less, in any case, than Homer's lines. From that severity of scholarship I ask leave to stand aside.

But the poem is greatest in that passage of it which, if the poet had been either Homer or Sophocles, if he had wished to obey any rules there may be either for tragic or for epic art, would not have been there at all; I mean, of course, the last eighteen lines of it. I will not say that the passage is too well known to quote; I have the hope that, because you know it, you will be willing to bear with it again. Keep before you the picture, and what has preceded. 'On the bloody sand Sohrab lies dead.' Rustum draws his cloak over his face, and sits by his dead son. You might think them two black granite pillars, 'once high-reared By Jemshid in Persepolis,' now 'prone, enormous.' Awhile the two armies stand at gaze; over the solemn waste slowly night descends, and the fog rises up off the Oxus. Then camp-fires are kindled,

and over the plain is borne the hum of the dispersing
armies; presently Rustum and his son are left alone
on the field:

> But the majestic river floated on,
> Out of the mist and hum of that low land,
> Into the frosty starlight, and there moved,
> Rejoicing, through the hushed Chorasmian waste,
> Under the solitary moon; — he flowed
> Right for the polar star, past Orgunje,
> Brimming, and bright, and large; then sands begin
> To hem his watery march, and dam his streams,
> And split his currents; that for many a league
> The shorn and parcelled Oxus strains along
> Through beds of sand and matted rushy isles —
> Oxus, forgetting the bright speed he had
> In his high mountain-cradle in Pamere,
> A foiled circuitous wanderer — till at last
> The longed-for dash of waves is heard, and wide
> His luminous home of waters opens, bright
> And tranquil, from whose floor the new-bathed stars
> Emerge, and shine upon the Aral sea.

So the poem ends; and to epic or tragic art, those
last lines are vanity. I think them, none the less, not
relevant merely, but an essential part of the poem to
which they belong; upon the tragedy that has gone
before, the perfect, and only possible, commentary.

To the sticklers for *kinds* in poetry, I will confess
plainly that I do not know just to what kind to relegate *Sohrab and Rustum*. But, if I did, of that kind, I
would say, it is the faultless example. You may like
some other kind better, you may seek qualities which
this poem has not, different and perhaps deeper qualities of the spirit; but you will not easily find work
more perfect, more instinct with harmony and propor-

tion, the parts of it more truly fused. Just what he set himself to do in this poem, Matthew Arnold has done, not less, nor more. If he had been questioned about it, I think he would have said, leaving aside all bother about kinds, that throughout the greater part of it he had endeavoured to carry to a modern reader some sense of the qualities that distinguish Sophoclean art: selective power in the disposition of a noble and moving story, a diction pitched to the grave quality of the theme, restraint both emotional and verbal, the harmonisation of all the elements of composition. This would touch only a part of the effects which characterise the poem: but a part not insignificant. Take that part, assume the purpose to be as I give it; what the poem seeks to do, it does with that degree of success which gives it a unique station in English poetry. *Sola Sophocleo tua carmina digna cothurno.*

I think it must please Matthew Arnold's ghost that the MS. of this poem, written in his own hand — a scholarly calligraphy — has its home today in Wordsworth's cottage in Grasmere.

In 1855 Matthew Arnold tried to repeat, with *Balder Dead*, the success of *Sohrab*. "I think *Balder*," he writes, "will consolidate the peculiar sort of reputation that I got by *Sohrab and Rustum*." But it was given to him, in this *epyllic* kind, to be great once, and thereafter to be only interesting. I will not spend too many words on his failure. But *Balder* is, in compass, his most ambitious piece; and it deserves that I should try and indicate some of the reasons why it failed. In the first place, Matthew Arnold took a story which could not easily be made interesting; for it contains no human personages; and it wants, not merely unity of action, but action of any kind. The first Book contains, certainly, the murder of Balder, the suicide of Hoder, and the mysterious sudden death of Nanna. But these dark happenings, which might seem to promise the interest, not merely of an epic, but of a detective novel, in fact serve only to set the scene for what follows; and what follows is not action, but description. They serve also, I may notice in passing, to give Matthew Arnold a taste for the word *corpse* which never leaves him — how many times he uses this horrible word I should not like to say. The second Book describes Hermod's journey to the dead, where he converses with Balder and Hela, and learns the terms on which Balder will be permitted to return to heaven. Balder will be given up if all the world can be persuaded to weep for him; a single recusant will be sufficient to bar his return. In the third Book these terms are recited to, and debated by, the gods; who make a pyre for Balder in the phrases of the 23rd Book of the Iliad, and light it with one eye upon the first paragraphs of *Beowulf*. Then all the world is bidden to weep for Balder. Odin, however, had all along suspected a trick — and there is one. Everybody is willing to weep except Thok. The reason why Thok will not weep is that she happens to be Lok in disguise — Lok who, all along, has been suspected of the murder of Balder. There is nothing left for it but that Hermod should make a second journey to the dead, and break to Balder the news that he must stay where he is — the reprieve-petition has failed. With Hermod's second conversation with Balder the poem ends.

The style of the poem does not want dignity, a rather prolix dignity, it may be. Seeking not merely severity, but plainness, it falls occasionally upon lines that are inert or stolid. But upon the whole we must marvel how rare these falls are, in a style which relies hardly at all upon the ornament of words. All the artifices of *Sohrab* are employed again. But the long-tailed similes drag their length a little wearily; some of them do not want suggestions of the grotesque. The damsel who guards the bridge over the Giall is elaborately compared with a waggon which gets into the way of a herd of cows. The dispirited looks of Hermod, returning from his journey, are likened to those of a farmer's dog who has lost his master and looks for him in the wrong house. Even the best of the similes, that which is used in Book I to describe the way in which Hoder brushes past Hermod in the dark, carries a more laboured art than its occasion warrants:

> And as a spray of honeysuckle flowers
> Brushes across a tired traveller's face
> Who shuffles through the deep dew-moistened dust,
> On a May evening, in the darkened lanes,
> And starts him, that he thinks a ghost went by —
> So Hoder brushed by Hermod's side . . .

Like Milton, Matthew Arnold knew how to make use of proper names. How effectively, to what insolent ends, he employs them in his prose-writings, no one can forget — Professor Pepper . . . Professor Frickel . . . he mentions them with all possible politeness, but at the breath of their own surnames they perish.[1] As he employs names for insolence in his prose, so he uses them for beauty in his verse. In *Sohrab* his Persian names serve him well enough; but the stiff-syllabled Scandinavian names with which *Balder* bristles he mouths to no purpose. Lidskialf and Breidablik and Igdrasil and Niflheim — these are place-names that do not come tripping on the tongue; perhaps one should not ask it of them; but it is difficult to love them; Niflheim especially, whose two syllables its poet consistently stretches to three, for scansion. He has better luck with some of the personal names, though I use myself with difficulty to such ungentle names, for female persons, as Aslauga and Angerbode; and I am perplexed with a Thok who is Lok, and a Frea the wife of Odin who is quite a different person from Freya the wife of Oder. I suppose it is not Matthew Arnold's fault that these names are what they are; that they are unfamiliar and deterrent. But at least it is his fault that we are not sufficiently interested in the story to take the names in the spirit in which they are offered. The poem does not live; and that is all about it. *Balder*, I am tempted to say, only comes to life when he is, not only dead, but buried — or rather burnt; when, in the last book, he

[1] Upon the subject of Matthew Arnold's use of personal names in his critical writings, see W. A. Raleigh's essay "Matthew Arnold" in *Some Authors*.

is already a ghost, a ghost in whose attenuated features the discerning reader finds surely the lineaments of his poet. The glory of *Sohrab* is its concluding paragraph (one glory among many, even so); the glory of *Balder* is the forty-five lines immediately preceding its last paragraph. Balder speaks: —

> For I am long since weary of your storm
> Of carnage, and find, Hermod, in your life
> Something too much of war and broils, which make
> Life one perpetual fight, a bath of blood.
> Mine eyes are dizzy with the arrowy hail;
> Mine ears are stunned with blows, and sick for calm,
> Inactive, therefore, let me lie, in gloom,
> Unarmed, inglorious; I attend the course
> Of ages, and my late return to light,
> In times less alien to a spirit mild,
> In new-recovered seats, the happier day.
>
> He spake; and the fleet Hermod thus replied: —
> Brother, what seats are these, what happier day?
> Tell me, that I may ponder it when gone.
> And the ray-crowned Balder answered him: —
> Far to the south, beyond the blue, there spreads
> Another heaven, the boundless — no one yet
> Hath reached it; there hereafter shall arise
> The second Asgard, with another name.
> Thither, when o'er this present earth and heavens
> The tempest of the latter days hath swept,
> And they from sight have disappeared, and sunk,
> Shall a small remnant of the gods repair;
> Hoder and I shall join them from the grave.
> There re-assembling we shall see emerge
> From the bright ocean at our feet an earth
> More fresh, more verdant than the last, with fruits
> Self-springing, and a seed of man preserved,
> Who then shall live in peace, as now in war.
> But we in heaven shall find again with joy
> The ruined palaces of Odin, seats

Familiar, halls where we have supped of old;
Re-enter them with wonder, never fill
Our eyes with gazing, and rebuild with tears.
And we shall tread once more the well-known plain
Of Ida, and among the grass shall find
The golden dice wherewith we played of yore;
And that will bring to mind the former life
And pastime of the gods, the wise discourse
Of Odin, the delight of other days.
O Hermod, pray that thou may'st join us then!
Such for the future is my hope; meanwhile,
I rest the thrall of Hela, and endure
Death, and the gloom which round me even now
Thickens, and to its inner gulph recalls.

That passage, and perhaps no other passage, certainly none of equal compass, sustains the high level of *Sohrab*. And it has a further interest. Matthew Arnold is commonly accounted a pessimistic poet; and in general, certainly, he attends his own funeral with the air of a man who is neither interested in the bakemeats nor excited about the resurrection. Against a general disposition in his poetry to expect no better immortality than that of being immortally melancholy, this passage may perhaps serve as offset. At least its sigh over human affairs is the sigh of a spirit that has sought and seen, in however distant a heaven, the heavenly light: quaesivit caelo lucem *ingemuitque reperta*.

Two years after the publication of *Balder* Matthew Arnold was elected to the professorship which he held continuously for ten years. At once he published *Merope*. It was "calculated," he says in a letter, "rather to inaugurate my professorship with dignity

than to move deeply the present race of humans."
But he believed in it; he did not withdraw it — it suf-
fered a worse fate, it was "remaindered" by its de-
sponding publishers; and it was nearly thirty years
before it was reprinted. It has merits more than professorial; it would not be Matthew Arnold otherwise.
Yet it is still fated to be read — where it is read — for
ends which I must call three parts professorial. Milton's marriage of classical form and Hebrew theme
leaves *Samson Agonistes* an equivocal example of the
art which it endeavours to represent; and *Merope*,
accordingly, may pass for the only considerable poem
in our language from which an English reader, a
reader, I mean, who has no Greek, and whose Latin
has never taken him to Seneca, can penetrate to a just
idea of the antique dramatic pattern. If the theme of
the poem had been, instead of a story which nobody
knows, one as familiar as Milton's, it would have had
better fortune. The action of it, even so, is more
surely managed than the characterisation; and into
the style there has been put too much of marble; a
marble not sufficiently often suffused with the colour
of a *human* beauty. Passages where that suffusion
takes place, such lines as these —

O Merope, how many noble thoughts,
How many precious feelings of man's life,
How many loves, how many gratitudes,
Do twenty years wear out, and see expire!
Shall they not wear one hatred out as well?

— lines instinct with that degree of feeling, are rather
rare.

Merope prompts me to ask a question to which I do not know the answer. Over a long period Matthew Arnold worked upon yet another tragedy taking its subject from antiquity. He dramatised the story of Lucretius. In 1866 he says that he had been "occupied" with it "for some twenty years." That takes us well back into the forties; and if I am right about that period, we can guess the interest he would have found in this mysterious legend of the philosopher and the love-potions. Was he working on the story when he wrote those fine lines in *The New Sirens*:

> Hath your wisdom felt emotions?
> Will it weep our burning tears?
> Hath it drunk of our love-potions,
> Crowning moments with the wealth of years?

It appears that he abandoned the poem when the *Lucretius* of Tennyson was published. But how far had it proceeded? What remains of it, and in whose keeping? I would give a good deal to see it; more than I would give to see — what has always excited the curiosity of scholars — the lost tragedy which Ovid wrote.

After the failure of *Merope* Matthew Arnold wrote very little poetry; not because of the failure of *Merope*; but *Merope* failed (if it did) for the same reasons as caused its author afterwards to write so little. In 1867, I may notice here, there was published in Cambridge the first American edition of his *Poems*. In the same year he concluded the decade of his Oxford professorship with a volume of *New Poems*. But the title, I have said already, was a little perverse. More than fifty pages of the book are occupied by a reprint of *Empedocles on Etna*; and with *Empedocles* are reprinted six other poems from the old *Empedocles* volume. The *Grande Chartreuse* stanzas, first printed in 1855, but written (if they were written among the scenes which they describe), not later than 1851; *Rugby Chapel*, finished in 1857; and *Dover Beach*, hardly composed later than the middle fifties — these three pieces are, after *Thyrsis*, the noblest poems in the book; no others, I think, can be ranked with Matthew Arnold's supreme work.

Thyrsis — which popular judgment, a judgment which, once again, I think true, puts above all other poems of Matthew Arnold — *Thyrsis* is certainly a late composition; and it is notable that it is at once so late and so great. How great I think it, I am almost afraid to say plainly. Mr. Robert Bridges puts it decisively below *Lycidas*. But he does so by finding in *Lycidas* a quality which either a dull ear or a hard heart obscures for me. For Mr. Bridges *Lycidas*, which to many of us seems a somewhat artificial composition, is essentially a passionate poem. I cannot think it that; or only so far as the poetical perception of beauty, only so far as all artistic perception, is passionate. Of passionate elegy our grand example is *Adonais*; yet with a passion, not personal, but cosmic. I wonder sometimes whether elegy should not have a little more of the warm kind earth about it. I wonder sometimes, indeed, whether the truest elegy in our language is not Cowley's poem on the

Death of Mr. William Harvey. I say, the truest, not the greatest. Of our four great elegies, at least it is the most natural and human, the human quality of it never obscured by ambitious effects of art or by philosophic reflection. It is noteworthy, I think, that three of these four elegies commemorate undergraduate friendships. It is noteworthy, again, that three of them are written in the pastoral manner.

Matthew Arnold was conscious that, in *Thyrsis*, he had too much left out Clough, that the man was not there, or that he had not made him sufficiently real. So conscious of that was he that he could not bring himself to send a copy of the poem to Mrs. Clough. But if he has not made Clough live for us, at least he has expressed, in the perfect art with which the Oxford countryside is delineated, a living scene. This truth of scene gives to *Thyrsis* an element of beauty wanting in our other great elegies. Thirteen years earlier, in *The Scholar Gispy*, Matthew Arnold had tried his hand upon the Oxford scene. If *Thyrsis* and *The Scholar Gipsy* had no other merits, yet their art in landscape, and the fine sentiment with which they particularise, with which they fix natural details — these two talents alone — might vindicate for Matthew Arnold a place with the greatest poets. Gray's *Elegy*, Collins' *Ode to Evening*, Keats' *Ode to Autumn*, it is with compositions of that supreme order that these two poems must be ranged.

The Scholar Gipsy belongs to the years 1852–53, Matthew Arnold's golden years. *Thyrsis*, which is a kind of sequel to it, has borrowed from those years some of their golden quality. It is much the greater of the two poems. Yet I doubt, if so late, at a time when his power in poetry was intermittent, Matthew Arnold could have achieved the supreme success of *Thyrsis*, were it not that the subject took him back to his *Scholar Gipsy* period, and to a period yet earlier, the period of his undergraduate youth. His power is lifted high by the immense inflooding of distant memories. The circumstances under which the poem was composed are, in any case, worth attention. Clough died in the November of 1861. Matthew Arnold was invited by the *Daily News* to contribute to its columns an obituary notice of him. "That I cannot do . . .", he writes. "But I shall some day in some way or other relieve myself of what I think about him." It was not until four and a half years later, not until 1865, that *Thyrsis* appeared in *Macmillan's Magazine*. In April of that year Matthew Arnold speaks of "the two years this poem has been forming itself" — all the while he was reading, he says, and re-reading, Theocritus. Five years lie between the poem and its occasion; two years were spent in the composition of it; thirteen years separate it from the poem to which it is the sequel. The principal defect of the poem is, I suppose, its too pervasive elegance. Even so I am not persuaded that it is a poem less great than any of the three with which it is natural to compare it. "Too quiet a poem for the general taste," Matthew Arnold writes of it; "but I think it will stand wear." With the last words he judged its character truly. I should make bold to say of it that it has "stood wear" better than any poem written in the last hundred years.

If I had to define Matthew Arnold's place in poetry, I should be disposed to say of him, quite simply, that he is the greatest elegiac poet in our language; not in virtue merely of *Thyrsis* — if anyone likes to think *Adonais* a greater elegy I am not overmuch disposed to quarrel with him — but in virtue of the whole temper of his Muse. His genius was essentially elegiac. Out of what experience we are to explain this dominant elegiac quality, it is not easy to know. I wish, I have said, that we knew more of the man, in the years which most matter. His poetry, profoundly melancholy, runs from the world, runs from it, as I think, hurt, hurt in some vital part. It believes itself able to sustain life only in the shade. The man himself we know only at that period of life when the poetry in him — the creative power, I mean, of the imagination — burns low. As we know him then, he appears a man not especially out of love with life. He speaks of himself somewhere as a worldly person: "the only worldly member of my family"; and to those who met him casually he did in fact seem worldly; fond of society, very much at ease in society; wanting altogether that quality of shyness without which no Englishman is thought quite complete; a scholar, perhaps; a gentleman unmistakably; on the whole, more of a gentleman than a poet has any right to be. There was about his urbanity an almost too fine finish; something gay to the point of insolence. Persons who respected him were pained by his flippancy. Someone asked him once, "Are you always quite serious?", and it was a question which only good manners prevented almost anyone from asking.

The contrast between the man, as he is scantly delivered to us, and the poetry which is the best part of him, is in truth somewhat remarkable. Yet after all, what do we go to the lives of great men for, what do we expect to learn, unless it be that they are not ordinary? The value of biography is in proportion as it deepens our sense of the paradox of human nature. Matthew Arnold had, I think, that worldly strain I speak of. It was made manifest in social intercourse; it shews itself in his prose writings; it peeps out occasionally, in a pleasant fashion enough, in his letters — of which, however, in general the most delightful quality is their even domesticity: they are much better letters than could have been written by a mere literary man or, if I may say so, by a mere poet. Of the wordly strain in him — I wish I could find some gentler term for it, less connoting moral blame — Matthew Arnold was, I think, conscious; and his consciousness of it was — from whatever causes — especially deep in the period of his best poetry. His best poetry stands deliberately aside from the world; that it should do so he conceived to be a condition of its life. The contrast between the superficial life of everyday and the buried life of the soul is dominant in his poetry to the degree of tyranny. "Lest the world have dominion over him" — that fear for ever follows him. In a sense, I suppose, the world did have dominion. In the critic, the educationalist, the theologian, the political disputant, the social star, more and more the poet became lost. His poetry, his great poetry, lies within narrow limits; limits so narrow that, seen carelessly, it fades to a point of reaction, a strong momentary reaction from a hurting worldly experience. That is not a just view of it; because, beyond those limits, it has a continuing if precarious life, over a considerable period of years; a life, however, drawing its best energy precisely from the consciousness in it of its own impermanence. Matthew Arnold's poetry owes its quality, its deeply affecting quality, to the power with which it expresses a spirit conscious that it is fighting, not a losing battle, but a battle against the world, in which the victory can, at best, be only hardly won. Always, there is "something that doth live"; and in the cause of it, repeatedly, he rallies his powers — "if that fails, fight as we will, we die!" The conception of poetry as a battle with worldliness, the worldliness in ourselves, and the worldliness in the world, is, I think, worth pondering—more particularly at the present time, when poetry has come to be thought easy, and the immortal garland is run for by persons who have not been at pains to submit themselves to a spiritual discipline. I do not think that the conditions of poetry are more easy today than they were fifty years ago. If the poetry of Matthew Arnold has something too much of what I have called "spiritual fussiness," at least he knew how hard it is to be a poet. It is hard to be a poet; it is harder still to stay one. We cry out upon recluses; we like a poetry which has stood in the winds of life. For my part, I like equally one which has sat in an ill-ventilated government office. It brings me nearer to the real problem. I am not sure that we always face the problem squarely. Is it certain that, under the conditions of our modern life, our life of cities, of making money, of being unable to make money, of the struggle, as the phrase is, to keep body and soul together, poetry, that is to say, the soul, has a chance? Is it certain that poetry does not demand a dedicated life? What dedicated life, you will say, had Shakespeare? I am not able to answer. But he was lucky, I feel, to come off with his soul.

✤✤✤✤✤✤✤✤✤✤✤✤✤✤✤✤✤✤✤✤✤✤✤

MATTHEW ARNOLD AS CRITIC

I HAVE lamented the declined vogue of Matthew Arnold's critical writings. When I was young and clever, he was the pattern of critical style and method. Today, I do not observe that young men read him; though I do not detect in them, as compared with the generation which they have supplanted, any falling off either in the art of being clever or the science of being young. Even when I was young, let me add, he never appealed to Scotchmen. I never knew why. Lamb said that he had been trying all his life long to like Scotchmen. I knew Scotchmen who tried hard to like Matthew Arnold; but none that ever made more than an indifferent success of it. It is not their want of humour. The most slashing attack upon Arnold's critical reputation which is anywhere to be found is in an essay by Walter Raleigh. Though a Scot, Raleigh had a quick and excellent humour. He was, moreover, as good a critic as we have had, since Matthew Arnold himself. Like Matthew Arnold, he was, in his best period, a professor in Oxford. Like Matthew Arnold, in the heart of him he despised Shelley; and they had other common sympathies. But Scotchmen do not like Matthew Arnold — and there is an end of the matter. In addition, Raleigh had a strong distaste for the saintly character. He was the son of a Scots minister. Born in the manse, sermons and expressions of piety vexed him pitiably.

In respect of Matthew Arnold, he could never rid himself of the feeling that the criticism of literature was being treated as though it were a part of the Church service.

There *is* that in Matthew Arnold; and there were persons other than Scotchmen whom it irritated. Mr. T. S. Eliot, in a recent essay, has instituted an elaborate comparison between Matthew Arnold and the late F. H. Bradley. When he left Harvard, Mr. Eliot betook himself to an Oxford college where he was near neighbour to Bradley, and indeed, under one roof with him. It happened to be my own college; so that I wonder whether Mr. Eliot ever heard Bradley — as I heard him more than once — delivering his soul upon Matthew Arnold. I cannot think so; or he would not have supposed that the two men had much in common. Matthew Arnold was the first professor of poetry in Oxford who was a layman. He was not only a layman, but a somewhat unbelieving one. He held that "miracles do not happen." He did not believe in a personal God, nor in a personal immortality. Of Christ he supposed the distinguishing character to be his "sweet reasonableness" — the kind of praise that you might bestow on Sainte-Beuve. But the heart of him, even so, was priestly. In his last years, he used to attend the chapel services at Harrow School. He was probably the only unbeliever in the congregation. But alone of the congregation he always insisted on turning to the East at the Creed. And this High-Church ceremonial manner he carried into literature; there is too much turning to

the East in his criticism. Bradley hated Matthew
Arnold's High-Church manner; and he hated still
more the Low-Church morality, or moralism, that
accompanied it. I recall the contempt with which he
used to speak of Matthew Arnold's lecture on Heine;
he had heard Matthew Arnold deliver it — and it is
certainly a rather incompetent performance. All this
would never have happened to Heine (you feel) if, at
the proper age, *he had been confirmed*. I like to think
that Mr. Eliot — so modern as he is (or was till
yesterday) — reads Matthew Arnold. But Bradley
had no patience with him; and is just so much like
him as any one Oxford man is like another — and no
more. It was an unlucky parallel. Mr. Eliot essays,
if I remember rightly, some comparison of the literary
styles of the two men — but, again, with wasted in-
genuity. The two styles stand contrasted as the
pointed and the diffused. I doubt if Matthew Arnold
ever wrote a *pointed* sentence — or Bradley any other
kind of sentence. I have a liking for epigram — I were
a prig else; but Matthew Arnold starves me of it.
Matthew Arnold is a great stylist who never made an
epigram. Bradley is an epigrammatist who never
made a great style. Both writers indulge, often, an
ironic manner. But how different they are, even
here: Matthew Arnold seeking his divine pattern in
Plato, Bradley a little earthy in his dependence upon
Gibbon and Voltaire.

But I mentioned Bradley and Mr. Eliot only to
indicate a certain sympathy which I have with those
persons who are offended by what may be called the

priestly and the moralistic elements in Matthew Arnold's criticism. I say "a certain sympathy"; for I am not prepared to carry it too far. I admit a tendency in Matthew Arnold to call no man a poet until he has been baptised and confirmed. He too much liked decorum, literary and moral. He preached too much, using too often the same texts. A man can have but one excuse for preaching — a religion. Matthew Arnold's religion was poetry — those of us who are so happy as to have better ones are, I suppose, the better for it. In the collapse of the creeds, Matthew Arnold took what he could get. "There is not a creed which is not shaken," he writes, "not an accredited dogma which is not shown to be questionable, not a received tradition which does not threaten to dissolve . . . most of what now passes with us for religion and philosophy will be replaced by poetry." Of whatsoever things are spiritual he supposed the greater part to be found in poetry. Deeply impressed by the consolations of poetry, he supposed the truths of it to illustrate life, attaching immense importance to moral truth. Of his dictum that poetry is a criticism of life I have spoken in an earlier lecture. I have never felt it to be absurd, but it can easily be made to seem so.

The absurd things that critics say live after them; and even of their gay half-truths the saving qualifications commonly perish with them. Matthew Arnold has the ill-luck to be best remembered by a travesty of his views on the relation between poetry and moral ideas, and by one or two bad misfires of critical

judgment. His judgments upon French poetry I
leave aside. But he preferred Shelley's letters to his
poetry; he thought Byron a better poet than either
Shelley or Keats or Coleridge. Worse than that, he
wanted the feeling for Burns; and yet worse, he was
unable to appreciate Chaucer. These judgments are
perhaps less remarkable than the method by which
they are reached. This may be called the method of
the *Frogs*. By the method of the *Frogs* I mean the
method which furnishes such admirable fooling in
Aristophanes' comedy of that name. In effect, it consists in selling poetry by the pound. Aristophanes
takes a pair of scales. Into the one scale he throws a
number of lines of Aeschylus, and into the other a
number of lines of Euripides. The better poetry consists of the lines which weigh heavier; the light stuff
is the cheap stuff. For the accuracy of the scales you
have to take the word of the critic. Matthew Arnold
operates this method, not like Aristophanes, with
partial seriousness and partial honesty, but really
trying to be honest with it and succeeding in being
serious. The method may be seen in its most elaborate employment in his essay upon *The Study of Poetry*.
There he takes (*inter alia*) a line of Dante, a line of
Chaucer, and — rather unfairly, but not meaning to
be unfair — two lines of Milton. He likes Chaucer's
line (as you knew he would) the least of all. That
might proceed from the circumstance that he misquotes it. But no! That you may not doubt his perfect impartiality, he misquotes, you will find, all three
authors. Having done that, he assures you gravely

that there is nothing like carrying with you everywhere, in your head or your heart, the great lines of
the great poets, and trying out against them the little
lines of the little ones. From the great lines, you will
get to know the "grand style."

However, even here Matthew Arnold achieved
something. He set people talking about the "grand
style." He had made a phrase. "You can still influence people," Disraeli said to him, "for you can
still make phrases." That has perhaps some touch of
cynicism — it were not Disraeli else. "The world is
still ruled by names," Gibbon had said, long before.
It is hateful, of course, that a writer should live by
purveying catchwords; and it is painful to feel that
one belongs to a public taken in by the way things are
said. We tell ourselves accordingly that nothing is so
precarious as the life of a catchword, and that literature is something better than phrase-making. So it is;
but even so I marvel at the life-saving quality of
good phrases — how often, at our great moral crises,
they come unsummoned, messengers of salvation to
weary and despondent souls. And indeed, if the
theory of style means anything, the matter of a good
phrase is some truth, or, what is sometimes more
wanted, some half-truth. Some of Matthew Arnold's
distinctive phrases — the "grand style," "high seriousness," "the free play of ideas," "sweetness and
light," "the best that has been known and thought in
the world"—these, I suppose, even today, when they
have forfeited their vogue, enjoy repute. It is easy to
speak of them as a kind of advertising captions; and

of Matthew Arnold as a singularly successful advertising agent for "Ideas." But after all, ideas are not
soap and cigarettes; and the truth is that with these
phrases of his Matthew Arnold did succeed in interesting an immense public in the subjects his
phrases summarise. It is perhaps good enough wit,
and certainly cheap enough, to speak of him as
"travelling in sweetness and light." That is, even so,
a sweet and light-bringing occupation. I suppose it
might be said of Carlyle that he travelled in moral
righteousness; or of Dr. Johnson that he travelled in
good sense. The truth is that we all travel, but most
of us get nowhere, and few of us deliver the goods.

Be this as it may, Matthew Arnold's phrases had,
while he lived, an immense and widely operative
vogue. In the vogue that they had, perhaps he took
too much pleasure. Yet he never troubled to make
his phrases too striking. Some of them are hardly
phrases at all. Most of them carry only just so much
of phrase as to serve the purpose for which they were
invented. The quality of them is, indeed, not so much
striking as caressive and flattering. And generally:
I know no other great writer who so much flatters the
vanity of his readers; each of whom, as he reads, is
sustained by the constant sense that he is acquiring
sweetness and light and that he is one of a very few
persons who are doing so. I suppose that the Athe-
nian sophists used similar arts of flattery, caressing
men into culture, and that that is a part of what Plato
objects against them. Just so much a sophist I will
concede Matthew Arnold to be; and it must, I suppose,

be accounted a kind of baseness to make men love knowledge for the good conceit of themselves which goes with it. But in a deeper sense, I will not agree that Matthew Arnold is a sophist — though unsophisticated persons have called him one. If I conceive rightly his aim in criticism, it was in fact the exact opposite of that of the sophists. For the crime of the sophists was precisely this; that they taught an interested love of knowledge. They taught, not a pure interest in ideas, but a love of ideas essentially related to practice, to politics, to party. The range of Matthew Arnold's interests was wide. Leave aside his defect of history — which is patent — and forget his contempt for science; not merely in literature, but in education, in politics, in religion, he was deeply interested and well informed. Literature was, I suppose, his first love; but if he had stayed there, he would not have been, I am inclined to think, a better critic than some others. Unless I mistake, it is precisely the interest which he had in education, politics, and religion which makes his criticism original. The value of literature lay, he supposed, in its power to furnish a temper of mind; to create that disinterested habit of intellect which secures for ideas a free play. Education, politics, religion, are immensely important subjects; to bring to them, not the prepossessions of pedantry, nor party spirit, nor fanaticism — all of which proceed from either ignorance or narrowness — but to set playing on these subjects minds habituated to free or liberal motions, minds nursed on ideas, minds informed by the best that has been known and thought among men — this is what is everywhere wanted, this is that soul's salvation which literature, and literature only, can work out in us. Of all that Matthew Arnold says upon Criticism that is the main substance. It is said with the most plainness and vigour in the first of the *Essays in Criticism;* but all the other essays say it again, or they say nothing. Something like it, of course, is said by other critics; something like it is said whenever the claim of ideas is pressed against the tyranny of any materialism. But the energy and bright persuasiveness with which Matthew Arnold urges his cause, the skill of temper which he lends to his plea, the variety with which he illustrates his single thesis — these things make him original.

The study of literature ends in a disposition of mind; its best gift to us is some faculty of spiritual freedom, a certain largeness of temper. No one, perhaps, — not even the mere aesthetician, — will be much disposed to quarrel with that. But Matthew Arnold goes somewhat further than that. He valued literature, I think, just in proportion as it creates the temper in which to view the great interests of life. He is not, I fancy, quite consistent with himself. Sometimes, for example, he seems to think of poetry as though its first business were to furnish anodynes for life. Occasionally, he concedes to it some rather sober power of joy. Very rarely, perhaps never in his heart, does he think of it as a pure source of pleasure, a delight among other delights. In the main, as I say, he values literature for the temper which it teaches —

poetry a temper of heart, prose a temper of the intellect; in either kind, the temper for looking at the great interests of life. For Matthew Arnold the great interests of life are the social and political and the religious. I think we too much forget how strong the obsession was with him, not merely of the religious interest, but of politics and the theory of society. Often enough, I know, he runs from politics — even from religion — to the consolations of poetry. Yet more often you might suppose him interested in literature only for its power to fit a man to judge questions of religion and social life. Indeed, if I am to mark him off as a critic from other critics, to find that in him which is individual, I can best do it, I think, by saying that beyond any other man of letters he valued the temper of the man of letters — conceiving it, not as an end in itself, but as an instrument of the art of living.

Of the temper of the man of letters he is himself, I must think, the fullest embodiment that our literature can shew. Last week,[1] I was bold to call Hazlitt the first of English critics, giving him, I said, a place which many people, perhaps most, would suppose to belong to Matthew Arnold. But I stand to what I said; and the more cheerfully that I think it possible to find first places for both my favourites. I am satisfied to call Matthew Arnold our greatest man of letters; and I add to that, what sounds a paradox, but is none, that he is a man of letters who became a literary critic by accident. We are so used to thinking of him

---

[1] See the lecture *Methods of Criticism in Poetry*, page 150. In order of delivery that lecture preceded the present one.

as a critic of literature, of poetry especially, and as a literary critic he achieved work of such distinction that we too easily forget how casual in fact were his connexions with this province. They were casual, intermittent, and in some respects not wholly congenial. If we leave aside a book which was published posthumously, the Second Series of *Essays in Criticism*,[1] Matthew Arnold has to his credit, in the department of literary criticism, only two books, one good, one bad. The good one is the *Lectures on Homer*; I think it may still pass for his masterpiece; and it was, in fact, his first book of criticism. The bad one — though it is impudent to christen so a book everywhere charmingly written, and full of interesting and stimulating criticism — the bad one is *The Study of Celtic Literature*. Matthew Arnold did not know enough about his subject; and generally not enough was known about the subject. The book remains, with all its merits, a rather useless performance. Neither of these books had any success — neither the good one nor the bad one: neither of them was reprinted during Matthew Arnold's lifetime. Both had, of course, an Oxford vogue — a thing which to a good many persons seems worse than no vogue at all. The Homer book was the first-fruits of Matthew Arnold's Oxford professorship; a professorship to which he had been elected, not because he was a critic, but because he was a poet. He was not a critic — he had written no criticism at all. In prose, he had to his credit a political pamphlet (now a

---

[1] The different Essays had been written, for the most part, between 1879 and 1888, and had appeared in literary periodicals.

bibliographical rarity) and two blue books — official publications of the Education Commission; one of these blue books he made into a real book. He took his blue books, let it be said here, always with great seriousness. What is more, they interested and influenced a wide public — one or two of them, reshaped into what I call real books, had a wider circulation than any of his purely literary works. Education, politics, religion — these, really (after poetry, which he abandoned very early), were his primary interest; these, and not the pure criticism of literature. Save for the accident of the Oxford professorship, I am not sure that it was in his heart to be a literary critic at all, as that phrase is most naturally understood. Certainly, he put his heart into the *Homer* Lectures; but the *Celtic Literature* is a little perfunctory — it was a part of a task, with not much more than curiosity behind it. Nor for the most part was Matthew Arnold's public interested in him as a literary critic. He first found himself, and the public first found him, and became interested in him, when he published the First Series of the *Essays in Criticism*. Perhaps one half of that book — or less — may be regarded as pure literary criticism. But already the religious interest is seen obtruding itself — in some of the essays inappositely. The best essays are those which indulge social, or politico-social, criticism. Of the literary essays not one, unless it be that on Heine, is concerned (save parenthetically) with a writer of the first class — the best of them is that on Maurice de Guerin; and of that the principal charm derives from Matthew Arnold's delicate touch in biography.

This book was followed, three years later (1867), by *Culture and Anarchy* — plainly called, this, in its title-page "An Essay in Political and Social Criticism." Political and social criticism was what the public wanted; and the book sold. I do not mean that it had an extravagant success on the Book Club scale. But while there was no demand at all for Matthew Arnold's purely literary essays, *Culture and Anarchy* and the first *Essays in Criticism* went through several editions. In style and manner *Culture and Anarchy* may, in any case, rank with Matthew Arnold's best work. I may notice that, though it was an essay in social and political theory, much of it had formed the substance of lectures delivered from the Oxford Chair of Poetry — a circumstance that may serve to indicate how roomy that Chair is.

But all the while that Matthew Arnold was thus mixing politics with poetics, he was moving towards a more dangerous occupation than either — theology. It has been found convenient to forget that it was by his theological writings that he first rose into the rank, or esteem, of a great writer. His first piece of pure theology was *St. Paul and Protestantism* — published in 1870. I have the fancy that of all his books this is, in some ways, the best written. Three years later appeared *Literature and Dogma*. I hate to reckon literary greatness by publishers' sales. But while Matthew Arnold's best book, the *Homer* Lectures, was, as I said, never reprinted in its author's lifetime, and while even his second-best book, the *Essays in Criticism*, took four years to reach a second edition, *Literature and Dogma* went through four editions in its first twelve months. Man is a political animal, says Aristotle. He is in some degree also a poetical one, though he rarely shews it. But above all, he is a theological one; and he shews it whenever you give him the chance.

A successful writer upon educational, political, and theological subjects — who had once written poetry which nobody read, and who from time to time wrote literary criticism which not very many people read — that, I think, would be a fair description of Matthew Arnold as he appeared to his contemporaries. In the last decade of his life he permitted editors and publishers to wring from him now and again a purely literary essay — perhaps a dozen such essays fall within this period; the best of them are the six that stand first in the posthumous Second Series of the *Essays in Criticism*. But they are casual and accidental glories — the by-products of a talent primarily interested in something else.

It is important to get this perspective. It is odd how often the world cares to remember us only by our by-products. Wisdom is no doubt justified of all her children; but she makes her best success very often of the illegitimate ones. Most of the questions in which Matthew Arnold was interested no longer interest anybody. His theological writings are, save so far as he is our only artist in theology, no longer vital. When he first wrote on education, there was none —

it is perhaps not his fault if there is now too much. How changed the face is of politics and society, I need not say; if there is any real break in the continuity of English political history, it falls between Matthew Arnold and ourselves, and not at the Rebellion or the Revolution. To questions of politics and society Matthew Arnold brought a strong anti-patriotic bias, which has ceased now to be irritating — who today thinks of preferring his own country to other people's? Upon all these subjects, however, Matthew Arnold was an extraordinarily effective writer. In connexion with them his writings will always be documents historically interesting; and, a hundred years hence, will seem perhaps more important than they are — from their pervasive readability and from their temper, the temper of a man of letters consistently looking at the world in the manner which literature has taught him.

For us, these merits have become not much more than interesting adjuncts to Matthew Arnold's proper fame, his fame as a critic of literature. As a critic of literature I rate him, after all deductions made, very high. Some of the deductions that have to be made I have already hinted, and others are obvious. I am not prepared to break my heart over the fact that he is not what is called a scientific critic. I am not offended by the circumstance that he not only shews no interest in, but in fact deprecates the use of, the historical method — the master-discovery of his age. I am not offended by it; nor surprised at it; for the truth is that Matthew Arnold was not a learned man — that was why he sometimes talked as though he knew everything. But he knew very little about the history of literature, and he liked to think (what may be true) that great poetry drops from the skies. In general, he indulges too much the appeal to absolute standards. He can as little tolerate that criticism should be personal as that it should be historical; and he loses a good deal here in warmth and colour. It is a habit of great poets, i. e., romantic poets, to seem not to belong to the world of books — to seem out of keeping with the serenities and decorums of literature. Expatiating in the Sacred Grove of poetry, Matthew Arnold hated to see human faces peeping out at him from behind the leaves — you could never tell when human nature, or the poetic nature, was not going to be malign, or even disreputable. Even so, he is not always consistent with himself; and in fact some of his best sketches are those in which the element of biography finds a place.

It is in a different way, I think, that Matthew Arnold disappoints us most. He thinks too much of the uses of literature, and too little of its pleasures. He attaches too much importance to taste, and too little to relish. By the waters of Helicon he sits down and sips, sampling them with the meticulous satisfaction of the wine-taster. It is horrible to see him, sometimes, tasting without swallowing. Nor in general has he, in appreciation, what I may call a good social manner. His criticism is tainted with a certain snobbery and even dandyism. All that is the defect, none the less, of a very real quality in him — he did believe

in the best, and he did know that it was not the
shoddy. Most of us do not; really, most critics do
not. Matthew Arnold's genuine flair for the best, the
insistency of his faith in the best, his pleasant manner
of sharing it only with the best men — a secret between you and him — these are first-rate virtues; and
not the less effective for an element which they have
of the *stagy*. For there *is* a good deal of the poseur in
him — I not only concede it cheerfully, but, to be
honest, I enjoy it. I like the good art of it, and the
supercilious airy amiability with which it is managed.
If Matthew Arnold carried into political and social
criticism the manner of a man of letters, he also carried into the criticism of literature — or liked to think
that he did — the air of a man of the world. The rôle
afforded him artistic delight; and on the whole it was
well suited to him. The part of it which he carries
least well is the cosmopolitan pose, the affectation of
being born on the continent. But in general his bland
finish of manner, and the delicacy of his irony, are
beyond praise. If he is not the greatest of English
critics, his make-up of being so is in itself a piece of
greatness; and not to enjoy it is a piece of stupidity.

Indeed, Matthew Arnold's real distinction, and the
best hope for him of a permanent fame in criticism, is
that he is so extraordinarily enjoyable. He is enjoyable almost everywhere; and a part of the enjoyment
is, if we are honest with ourselves, the delight which
we derive from a finely adjusted pose. I am not sure
that we have not too much outgrown what I would
call the simpler pleasures of literature — it is part and

parcel of a general sophistication. But I will not be put off by it. Because others are sophisticated, I am not going to be ashamed to say that, after the fashion of the period in which I was born, I value literature very largely by the enjoyment which I derive from it. I am delighted in Matthew Arnold by what I feel to be the pervasive charm of his temper — it is not the less charming to me from the affectations that go with it. The style of mind, the manner, delights me — as an artistic product it delights me. And yet again, and finally, and yet more in the fashion of yesterday, I enjoy above all things Matthew Arnold's beautiful English. Here again, some affectations that I am aware of do not hurt me — I think they enhance my satisfactions. Perhaps Matthew Arnold's style a little lacks masculinity; at least the he-men of litera-ture do not write like this. Yet it has qualities which we shall be hard put to it to match in any others of our prose-writers. For a like delicacy of prose-style, for a prose equally characterised by symmetry and proportion and harmony, we are driven to French literature or to the ancient Greek. I hate to speak of truth of style — it opens the floodgates for bad meta-physic or for cant. But, properly guarded, the phrase does mean something. In Matthew Arnold's beauti-ful English I seem to myself always to find both grace and truth. Grace and truth are qualities rare, I suppose, in any age. Our own age wants grace per-haps more than truth. We *have* a kind of ugly truth-fulness. But we too little esteem grace — and we have ceased to read Matthew Arnold.

✿✿✿✿✿✿✿✿✿✿✿✿✿✿✿✿✿✿✿✿✿✿✿

EMERSON

I AM told that Emerson has less honour in his own country than he once had. I cannot judge that; but if it be true I can think of many reasons for it, reasons having their ground in conditions not peculiar to America, but operating today all over the world. In England, he is certainly not widely read — I think he never was, but he is less read today than he was thirty years ago. In Oxford, if I am caught reading him, it is as though I were caught reading the Bible. I am reckoned with those morbid eccentrics, the dead who bury their dead. Nor is Emerson thought to have died very honourably; for, as the epitaph of him is written in England, he some time since died one death with Carlyle.

How dead Carlyle is it would be difficult to say. He has never been a "favourite" with me; he never caught my youth. I observe, therefore, dispassionately, and in the spirit of one merely recording facts, that he neither holds nor catches the youth of today. Among young men, as I find them around me, abounding in every kind of literary enthusiasm, not deterred by interests the most bizarre, I have yet to stumble upon an enthusiast for Carlyle. In a world that has made up its mind to be done with shams (for it is that, surely, which gives its character to the age we live in, and which makes it so interesting, sometimes so alarming), in a world that hates all shams, this professional hater of shams goes unregarded. I am not sure that he is not accounted himself one of the many shams of that sham-great age (so it is conceived), the Victorian. Of that age, of which so many of the glories have become obsolete, I take the imperishable and untarnishable glory to be the crusade which it led against superstition. Over many of the vaunted effects of Victorianism, Time has drawn the sponge with rude hand; but the work done by the great Victorian scientists retains a singular permanence of outline. Some of them, men like Huxley and Tyndall, drew from Carlyle a large part of their inspiration. From Carlyle they conceived themselves to have learned sincerity. Today they look more sincere than he does. Of all the Victorian reputations his has worn, perhaps, worst. Sixty years ago, he was a kind of religion. Today he is, what he most hated, a superstition; a superstition only differing from others in the circumstance that no one is prepared to die for it.

In England, it has been Emerson's fate to be thought of always in connexion with Carlyle — Charles Eliot Norton must bear some of the blame of that. In an earlier lecture, I mentioned the disparaging terms in which Wordsworth speaks of him. To Emerson himself Wordsworth confided that he "sometimes thought Carlyle mad." To Mr. Reed he confided that he thought Emerson an inferior Carlyle. That view of Emerson was aired, you will remember, by Mrs. Carlyle. And there is undoubtedly an element of Carlylese in Emerson. He has something of Carlyle's prophetical pose. If he does not wear the Carlyle girdle of camel's-hair, at least he affects a diet of wild honey. His style, again, has faults, some of which (though not so many as is believed) are plainly traceable to Carlyle. Carlyle's best power he wants — the painter's "devouring" hand and eye, the historical canvas staring you into credence. He would be better, perhaps, if he had something of Carlyle's sardonic quality; he would not then so often be led to the wrong side of that narrow border which demarcates genius from quackery. But enough in any case connects him with Carlyle to make it natural that, in the decline of Carlyle's fame, he should suffer some diminution of repute. His repute, his English repute I mean, came to him out of the same conditions as gave vogue to Carlyle. His power found its first opportunity in the collapse in England of Newmanism, of what is called the Oxford Movement. The failure of Newmanism left in England "a whole population of ladies and gentlemen" — I use a phrase of Emerson's — "a whole population of ladies and gentlemen out in search of religion." But hardly had the first wave hit them than the second fell; in the crash of it, faith itself, and not merely some one form of it, seemed to reel. Swift upon the disaster of Newmanism followed "the huge displacement caused by the tidal wave of the Darwinian idea." [1] Both Carlyle and Emerson brought to the disillusioned Newmanists fresh religious hope.

---

[1] I borrow this phrase (with the proper apologies) from a source which I am now no longer able to trace.

And in the second, and greater, disaster of faith it was given to them still to speak courage to the terrified hearts of men.

Emerson visited Oxford in 1847. He met there both Clough and Matthew Arnold. Who had first brought his writings to their notice I do not know — was it Harriet Martineau, who in 1836 had visited Emerson at Concord? Clough and Matthew Arnold had listened, as undergraduates, to the preaching of Newman:

Moor the vessel with a thread of silk; cleave the granite rock with a razor's edge; as little may you hope, with the keen and delicate instruments of human reason and human foresight, to contend against those giants, the passion and the pride of man.

That is Newman — a characteristic sentence, shaped with that fine sense which he had of the power of harmony to lull thought. That is Newman, with nothing of doctrinal about it, truly; but receive it, and from it flows all doctrine. Put against it a voice of different tone, but with not less of music in it. Take almost any sentence of Emerson in which he is most like himself. I choose almost at random, but these sentences will do:

As men's prayers are a disease of the will, so are their creeds a disease of the intellect.

It is only as a man puts off all foreign support, and stands alone, that I see him to be strong and to prevail.

I see not any road of perfect peace which a man can walk but after the counsel of his own bosom.

To men who had heard Newman, who had listened
to preaching of which the sum was that, in the counsel
of his own bosom, in human reason, never should a
man find peace, here — or in any of Emerson's characteristic oracles — was that order of utterance
which might well seem life-giving. This was a new
and strange voice, a "voice oracular" Matthew
Arnold calls it, a voice speaking (so it seemed to him)
of life unto the dead. Matthew Arnold's lecture upon
Emerson is well known. In that lecture he has spent
the best beauty of his prose in recalling what Newman meant to his undergraduate youth, and what
Emerson meant. When he wrote it, he was sixty.
But go back to his twenties, and to his poetry, to the
sonnet which he wrote in his copy of Emerson's
Essays:

"O monstrous, dead, unprofitable world,
That thou can'st hear, and hearing, hold thy way!
A voice oracular hath pealed today,
Today a hero's banner is unfurled;

Hast thou no lip for welcome?" So I said,
Man after man, the world smiled, and passed by:
A smile of wistful incredulity,
As though one spake of life unto the dead:

Scornful, and strange, and sorrowful; and full
Of bitter knowledge. Yet the Will is free;
Strong is the Soul, and wise, and beautiful:

The seeds of godlike power are in us still:
Gods are we, bards, saints, heroes, if we will! —
Dumb judges, answer, truth of mockery?

A voice oracular. Yet not announcing, it would
seem, truths particularly new; and some of its propo-

sitions even disputable — for the will may be free,
but it behaves as though it were not: I speak as one
not bred in Calvinist Massachusetts; and the matter
is, in any case, not so simple as Matthew Arnold
would have it. "The gate of gifts closed on us at our
birth"; that is one of Emerson's favourite oracles.
And again: "Let us build altars to the Beautiful
Necessity." But the two best lines of Matthew
Arnold's sonnet do sum adequately the main tenour
of the book they commend:

> Strong is the Soul, and wise, and beautiful,
> The seeds of godlike power are in us still.

But is that all? For that must two Oxford students
"out in search of religion" go so far abroad? The
truth is, they need not go abroad at all. Quite the
opposite: "Let a man go home," says Emerson.

I do not know how often he does not say it; like one
of those Greek oracles that kept on giving the same
response, some direction so simple that the recipient,
seeking a deep meaning, missed the plain one, and
came back to the shrine for something better — for
we are always expecting the Divine Wisdom to be
more profound than our occasions warrant.

In his lecture upon Emerson, Matthew Arnold is
immensely ready to give up to Time all of Emerson
which Time can fairly claim. He gives up — for he is
a critic genuinely disinterested — he gives up Emerson's poetry. He gives up what, if it were better than
it is, he would still not have understood (for he was
the least metaphysical of men), his philosophy. And

what does he leave? Like two other bad philosophers,
like St. Paul, like Marcus Aurelius, Emerson is a great
"friend and aider of those who would live in the
spirit." With any of that, so far as it goes, I have not
much quarrel. It is with a true and fine instinct, I
think, that Matthew Arnold places Emerson with
those other two. But there his insight stops; or he
sends it no further than to chase generalities upon the
subject of Emerson's serenity, his hopefulness, his
sweetness. The conditions of his qualities, the hiding-
places of his power, he does not explore.

About Emerson's poetry I am going to say little or
nothing, and certainly nothing that is new. That his
station is not with the greatest poets needs, I shall
suppose, no arguing. Yet I think him a better poet
than he is commonly accounted — it is not a little
discreditable to us that such a poem as *Threnody*
should not be known wherever English is spoken. At
least Emerson comes of a high and interesting poetical
lineage. He is in the true succession of the metaphysical poets. *Parnassus* and the Preface to *Parnassus* bear witness to his interest in Donne and
in Crashaw; and without *Parnassus* that he had
studied to good purpose both Herbert and Cowley,
to say nothing of Ben Jonson, is plain from his
poetry. To these poets he owes his contempt for
the conventional poetical diction, to these that bias
towards the *odd*, that singularity, which so much dis-
tinguishes his verse. Another strain is, I suppose, the
Persian. Yet how "Persian" already is such a poet
as Cowley! To the habit, however, of reading Persian

poetry in translation — and of reading in translation a great deal of other poetry [1] — may be traced, I fancy, at least some of the defects of Emerson's verse. It led him to suppose that an idea could look after itself. Not only was it so far independent of words that it could come through from one language to another with its substantial force very little impaired, but Emerson came near to persuading himself sometimes that words were a kind of fine dress which the manhood of a beautiful or just idea could do without. It is this prepossession, as I believe, that is responsible for the untidiness of so much of his verse. His best power lies in epigram; but in that kind of epigram which relies for its effect always upon the thought, and never upon the words — the idea is fine enough, or sharp enough, to look after itself: of verbal art there is almost nothing, but everything depends on a kind of sleight of mind. Between epigrams [2] Emerson seems sometimes to be hardly a poet at all. In almost any poem of some compass, you may observe him, over initial tracts of dull or untidy work, fumbling towards his epigram, groping uncertainly towards the point of light. As often as not, when he finds it, he dies upon it; he falls back into dullness; or the flash

[1] See what is said on this subject in the essay "Books" (in *Society and Solitude*). The only poet who must be read, and who cannot be read in translation, is, that essay suggests, Martial. It is notable that, of Latin poets, the essay reckons as indispensable only Martial and Horace. Virgil is not so much as named, nor Catullus nor Lucretius. All this suprises you if you have not read Emerson's poetry; if you have, it still surprises you, but not very much.

[2] The term epigram is unsatisfactory; the Latin term *sententia* would do better. (See below, page 103.)

suffices to irradiate a paragraph; and then begins a new darkness, a new fumbling. The truth is that, dealing so widely in epigrammatic ideas, having usually so much luck with them, Emerson forgot that, while these can look after themselves, the main stuff of ideas in a poem of any extension is of a less self-sufficing order. This makes him careless both of language and of rhythm; and the tendency to respect both these elements of verse less than they deserve was the stronger in him for yet another reason. He was inclined everywhere too much to emphasise that character of poetry which consists in the escape from custom. Any trimness of art offended him as a part of customariness.

The flight from custom makes him often singularly wilful. From many parts of his poetry you might suppose the imagination to have no other exercise than the ranging of thesis and antithesis. Such a poem as that entitled *Character* has come into being for the delight of that exercise, and seems to end only when the mind is tired with it:

> The sun set, but set not his hope;
> Stars rose; his faith was earlier up:
> Fixed on the enormous galaxy,
> Deeper and older seemed his eye;
> And matched his sufferance sublime
> The taciturnity of Time.
> He spoke, and words more soft than rain
> Brought the age of gold again:
> His action won such reverence sweet
> As hid all measure of the feat.

So far as that goes, it could hardly be better. But it could hardly go further, perhaps, without falling into triviality. From the triviality which is the bane of so much of the metaphysical poetry, the poetry of Emerson, it is fair to say, is mostly saved by the moral ardour which informs it. It is strange, even so, how the moral ardour in him seems able to express itself only in the explosion of epigram. In what a fine fire it often goes up, I do not need to say: "So nigh is grandeur to our dust . . .," "'Tis man's perdition to be safe. . . ." — I need not cite verses which everybody knows. It is not altogether true, but it is, I think, mainly true, that Emerson's inspiration rarely climbs higher than the couplet or the quatrain. Nor can I forbear to suggest that the effects which some of his best quatrains achieve are often of a kind which he compasses even better in his prose. I will illustrate what I mean by placing side by side two epigrams, so far similar that they are both epitaphic, but the one verse, the other prose. Here is, firstly, his epitaph on Samuel Hoar, in a manner pleasantly reminiscent of Landor:

> With beams December planets dart
> His cold eye truth and conducts scanned,
> July was in his sunny heart,
> October in his liberal hand.

Wholly delightful. But place beside it, from his prose, this upon Lincoln: "His heart was as great as the world, but there was no room in it to hold the memory of a wrong." Ransack the *Greek Anthology*; you will hardly better, out of it, *that!* Prose it is. But can poetry do better? Does the poetry of Emerson often, or ever, do as well?

Though Emerson's best poetry is, I think, in the
metaphysical kind, it is proper to notice that one
or two of his noblest successes are scored in a different kind, a kind almost plain. Such poems as *The
Rhodora*, *The Two Rivers*, and the Concord Monu-
ment *Hymn*, reach, in a quite different style, effects
either beautiful or noble. It is perhaps not without significance that none of these three pieces is
composed in the metre which Emerson uses elsewhere
in preference to any other. The great body of his
verse is written in a metre, the rhymed octosyllabic,
which, if it is the oldest of English measures, has not
become more manageable with time — it is a metre
which has never failed to take full vengeance upon
poets who use it without art or with disrespect.
Emerson shews it every kind of disrespect, disorder-
ing his rhymes and his lengths and the verse-empha-
sis; but almost never with a happy boldness; nearly
always he pays heavily for his adventure, his *morale*
deteriorating with each fresh indulgence of whim.
Nowhere, I feel, has he the true sense of this metre;
and it is his unlucky addiction to it, as much as anything else, that bars him from the highest successes of
poetry. With yet another metre, I am obliged to add,
he is even more unfortunate. In *The Adirondacs*
and in one or two of his shorter poems, he essays
blank verse. *The Adirondacs* aspires after Words-
worthian quality; but not the worst of Wordsworth,
perhaps, is quite so incompetent, poetically, as that
part of Emerson's poem which celebrates the laying
of the first Atlantic cable. Yet the worst incompe-

tence of the poem is the metrical; Emerson has learned not so much as the elements of his measure. No tyro ever placed his pauses with so little skill.

In general, Emerson's poetry is too *curious*. I prefer that word to some others. I do not like to say that it is too philosophical. The mind is at work in it, certainly; yet not in the mountainous Pelion-upon-Ossa fashion of constructive intellect. The truth is that Emerson is not a philosopher at all, as that word is understood today; he is not so either in his poetry or in his prose. On the other hand, his gifts have considerable likeness to those of the class of persons called in the eighteenth century *natural philosophers*. I am surprised if a large part of the success which he has in prose does not proceed from the qualities of the naturalist in him. When, in 1833, he gave up preaching for lecturing (if indeed he ever did give up preaching), his first lecture was upon *The Uses of Natural History*. But he was a naturalist only in a special field. "The natural history of man," he says, "has never been written. . . . The philosophy of six thousand years has not searched the chambers and magazines of the soul." When he was in England he gave a course of lectures, much of which he repeated in Harvard in his old age, on *The Natural History of the Intellect*. That is his field; he is a naturalist of the soul of man — a naturalist of inspired industry, watchful for each small detail of the soul's life, observing with a quick and fine eye its subtlest reactions upon all variety of contacts, interpreting with penetrative intelligence data the most doubtful, con-

ducting the results of loving observation, sometimes
overconfidently, towards a unifying principle.

The unifying principle is to be found, of course, in
the doctrine of the Oversoul. I can see Matthew
Arnold shy at that; scenting metaphysic from afar;
and not, like the horse when he scents battle, in the
book of Job, neighing victoriously; but I see him di-
lating the nostril of a nervous dilettantism, not quite
sure whether he can slay his enemy merely by disliking the smell of him. Well, the Oversoul has musty
origins, not too Anglo-Saxon either; though if a man
cares to go to Coleridge for just that in Coleridge
which makes some people think him a charlatan, he
will find airs and floating echoes of Oversoulism. Like
Coleridge, Emerson was always getting into philosophy; but, in God's providence, he had, what
Coleridge lacked, a happy gift of getting himself out
again. I will not say that the poet in him plucks back
the charlatan; yet there was that in him which made
all sorts of quackeries tempting to him, and he liked
to put his head over the garden-wall; but always a
canny American genius drags him back by the coat-
tails. The simplest way of reassuring ourselves about
the Oversoul is to be persuaded that nothing that
Emerson says about it is different at all from what
wise men, that is, poets, have always said about the
Soul. If our souls were our own, we should not make
so much fuss about them; if they were only ourselves,
we should not be aware of their presence. If we did
not share one soul with all mankind, life would not be
that affair of passions and desires that it is. If there

were no soul in nature, or not our soul, out of nature
we should never have emerged. At obvious verities
such as those, not at anything more difficult, Emerson aims all that he says; and we are as frightened of
it as though we did not know what it meant:

That great nature in which we rest, as the earth lies in
the soft arms of the atmosphere; that unity . . . within
which every man's particular being is contained and made
one with all other; that common heart, of which all sincere
conversation is the worship, to which all right action is sub-
mission; that overpowering reality which confutes our
tricks and talents, and constrains every one to pass for
what he is, and to speak from his character, and not from
his tongue, and which evermore tends to pass into our
thought and hand, and become wisdom, and virtue, and
power, and beauty. We live in succession, in division, in
parts, in particles. Meantime within man is the soul of the
whole; the wise silence; the universal beauty, to which
every part and particle is equally related; the Eternal One
. . . I dare not speak for it. My words do not carry its
august sense; they fall short and cold. Only itself can inspire whom it will, and behold! their speech shall be lyrical,
and sweet, and universal as the rising of the wind.

I protest, all that is as simple as it could be. If we
do not understand it, it is not because we want philosophy, it is because we want poetry. But in case it
seems less simple than it is, let me elucidate it from
the first sermon that Emerson ever preached, a sermon which goes back to 1826, when he was three-
and-twenty, but yet contains in germ his whole doctrine of the Soul and of the unity of the spiritual and
natural worlds. A farm-labourer on his uncle's farm

observed to him one day that "men were always praying, and that all prayers were granted." From this Emerson drew an important conclusion which he was bold to make the basis of his first sermon. All prayers are granted: "we must beware, then, what we ask." We are one being with God and the world; whatever we will, therefore, happens. From that follows, for Emerson, the whole moral law. Whatever a man is, thinks, or says, the shock of it is felt through the totality of nature. So great, no less, is the responsibility of the soul before the universe. The subject of prayer is but one illustration of the doctrine of the One Soul. But in the *Essay on Self Reliance* it affords Emerson a passage of lofty eloquence which I may perhaps be allowed to quote here:

In what prayers do men allow themselves! That which they call a holy office is not so much as brave and manly. Prayer looks abroad, and asks for some foreign addition to come through some foreign virtue, and loses itself in endless mazes of natural and supernatural, and mediatorial and miraculous. Prayer that craves a particular commodity — anything less than all good — is vicious. Prayer is the contemplation of the facts of life from the highest point of view. It is the soliloquy of a beholding and jubilant soul. It is the spirit of God pronouncing his works good. But prayer as a means to effect a private end is meanness and theft. . . . As soon as the man is at one with God, he will not beg. He will then see prayer in all action. The prayer of the farmer kneeling in his field to weed it, the prayer of the rower kneeling with the stroke of his oar, are true prayers heard throughout nature, though for cheap ends. . . . As men's prayers are a disease of the will, so are their creeds a disease of the intellect.

To that passage let me add two sentences from the first book that Emerson ever published, the little volume entitled *Nature*: "Is not prayer also a study of truth — a sally of the soul into the unfound infinite? No man ever prayed heartily without learning something." I have called Emerson a naturalist. But the study of nature, natural philosophy, and ndeed all learning, is, as he conceives it, a kind of prayer. Prayer is the articulation of our curiosities. Observation, experiment, verification — the naturalist's trinity of excellence — all these are governed by prayer. Emerson will, in fact, never allow that there is such a thing as a mere naturalist; the naturalist, he says somewhere, "must be a poet in his severest analysis." When I call Emerson a naturalist, therefore, I surround the term with those qualifications which he himself supplies. The term so qualified does, I think, serve to differentiate him, to mark off his greatness from that of other great writers to whom he seems most like. St. Paul is not a naturalist, Marcus Aurelius is not a naturalist. Of neither do the first motions proceed from the instinct of natural enquiry, nor does either use the method of the naturalist. Not only does Emerson approach his subject, the human soul, in the *curious* spirit of the natural philosopher, but equally with his temper his method is that of the naturalist; and it is this which gives to his idealism that practical turn which it has. I have called him, what I think he is, and what most idealists are not, *canny*. His subject is the soul. But he goes down on his hands and knees to it; grubbing about it with en-

joyment, and with something of the earth upon him
when he rises. The primary business of the naturalist
is observation; the observation frequently of minute
particulars; the observation of these, and then the
storing and classification and ticketing of them. That
Emerson is best in short sentences has been said again
and again — I fancy, indeed, too often. Those short
sentences ticket his observations; they pin and label
his specimens of the soul's behaviour. Of aphorism
and apophthegm he is one of the greatest masters in
literature; the equal, I think, of Seneca. Each of his
aphorisms or apophthegms is a kind of card or label,
disposing in perfection for the light, as it were, some
rare *lepidopteron*, some fine wing or feather of spiritual
fact.

But I have not done with Emerson when I have
called him an inspired naturalist of the human soul.
He is in fact also a great literary artist. It is to this
side of his work, as I think, that justice is least often
done. At the moment, indeed, I can recall no one,
unless it be William James, who has said plainly,
what is, I think, bare truth, that Emerson's greatness
is pre-eminently that of a verbal artist. Matthew
Arnold does not say it; and to hear it would have hor-
rified him. In fact he hardly thinks of Emerson as a
man of letters at all — he is a St. Paul, a Marcus
Aurelius; of that order of writers, therefore, to whom
literature is vanity. And some of Emerson's utter-
ances encourage this view of him. "Converse," he
says, "with a mind that is grandly simple, and literature looks like word-catching." Yet the artist in him,

the artist in words, *was* dominant — exiled from his verse to be the tyrant of his prose. Such a word-watcher, such a word-catcher, such a weigher-in-the-balance of niceties of rhythm and order, as well as of phrase, has seldom been.

Epaminondas, brave and affectionate, does not seem to us to need Olympus to die upon, nor the Syrian sunshine. He lies very well where he is.

O friend, never strike sail to a fear. Come into port greatly, or sail with God the seas.

What makes the majesty of the heroes of the senate and the field, which so fills the imagination? The consciousness of a train of great days; and victories behind. . . . That is it which throws thunder into Chatham's voice, and dignity into Washington's port, and America into Adams's eye.

I have avoided the sentences oftenest quoted — I am concerned at the moment with those which have most of literary artifice. "Thunder into Chatham's voice, and dignity into Washington's port, and *America into Adams's eye*" — that *America*, that sudden turn-away, giving you — when you expect, to match Chatham's *thunder*, a natural power, *lightning*, and some moral quality to balance the *dignity* of Washington — instead of these, giving you a *whole continent* of qualities, qualities the most precious to the hearer, *all America* in the glance of one man; that surely is the rhetorical art in its fullest capacity. Drawn, if you like, not from the tongue, but from character; yet it is art even so. Epaminondas, again: "He lies very well where he is" — is the very special effectiveness of that luck or art?

I have deprecated the criticism which ties Emerson to short sentences, and supposes him constitutionally unable to string two sentences together. His prose, like his verse, is best, no doubt, in what is properly called the sentence, in what the Latins, I mean, understood by the word *sententia*, in the moral aphorism, in that kind of epigram which, in so far as it aims rather at the affections than at the mind, deserves some better name. These sentences shine in the *Essays*, often with a solitary light, lonely stars of thought. Often, however — and far more often than in Emerson's verse — the fine point of light relieves its own concentration in a kind of star-burst, propagating itself across whole paragraphs — paragraphs which become glowing and luminous. This order of effect I may be allowed to illustrate from the concluding paragraphs of the Essay on "Heroism" — of the first sentence I have made use already:

I see not any road of perfect peace which a man can walk, but after the counsel of his own bosom. Let him quit too much association, let him go home much, and stablish himself in those courses he approves. The unremitting retention of simple and high sentiments in obscure duties is hardening the character to that temper which will work with honor, if need be, in the tumult or on the scaffold. Whatever outrages have happened to men may befall a man again; and very easily in a republic, if there appear any signs of a decay of religion. Coarse slander, fire, tar and feathers, and the gibbet, the youth may freely bring home to his mind, and with what sweetness of temper he can, and enquire how fast he can fix his sense of duty, braving such penalties, whenever it may please the next newspaper and a sufficient number of his neighbors to pronounce his opinions incendiary.

It may calm the apprehension of calamity in the most susceptible heart to see how quick a bound nature has set to the infliction of malice. We rapidly approach a brink over which no enemy can follow us. "Let them rave: Thou art quiet in thy grave." In the gloom of our ignorance of what shall be, in the hour when we are deaf to the higher voices, who does not envy those who have seen safely to an end their manly endeavor? Who that sees the meanness of our politics, but inly congratulates Washington that he is long already wrapt in his shroud and for ever safe; that he was laid sweet in his grave, the hope of humanity not yet subjugated in him? Who does not sometimes envy the good and brave who are no more to suffer from the tumults of the natural world, and await with curious complacency the speedy term of his own conversation with finite nature?

I cannot think *that*, in its sustained heroic character, the work of a man great only in gasps; and to the nobly diffused eloquence of it it would be easy to find parallels from many parts of Emerson's prose writings. Above all I am impressed by the *verbal art* of it. The Essay upon "Heroism," from which the passage is taken, is one of the best in the *Essays* of the *First Series*. All of them are good, save perhaps two, the Essays upon "Friendship" and "Love." Those I think the weakest; they were written, we can hardly doubt, the first of them when Emerson was very young,[1] the second when he was trying to be so. But for the *Essays* of the *First Series* as a whole I

---

[1] Mr. Russell's *Emerson: the Wisest American* puts this Essay (and, I think, the poem *Etienne de la Boece*) in its proper connections.

EMERSON   105

want to plead that, not only has each of them in-
dividually more development in its ideas, better managed connexions, than is usually allowed, but the
series itself is a developing series — I feel this the
more with each re-reading. The *Essays* should be
read in the order in which Emerson placed them. So
read, each succeeding Essay makes what preceded
better understood; till gradually whatever appeared
at first dark or difficult in the thought "defecates to a
pure transparency." The *Second Series*, so far as it
has less extravagance of both sentiment and style, will
be thought by some critics better, by others disap-
pointing, according as we believe in, or mistrust, the
spirit of youth. It is in some respects more original;
for in it the *canny* quality of Emerson's idealism first
becomes strongly marked. The *Essays* lie between
Nature and *The Conduct of Life*. I have known critics
who thought either of these better than the *Essays*.
For myself, I feel that *Nature* has not found, *The Conduct of Life* does not everywhere keep, Emerson's
essential quality. It is wonderful, even so, how fresh
Emerson keeps his wisdom — and his art of words —
into late years. The free speculative temper never
leaves him. The volume of 1860 contains work as free
in temper and as imaginative as the first *Essays* or the
earlier *Man Thinking*.

I cannot leave Emerson without directing attention
to a merit in him which makes him nearly everywhere
delightful to read, one for which we give him less than
due credit because it seems, perhaps, less a literary
than a social grace. Hardly any writer that I know,

who has so many good things of his own, is equally
full of other people's good things. His works, take
them where you will, are a storehouse, singularly rich,
of great sayings and great actions picked from all
parts of history and from an astonishingly wide range
of literature — east and west, yesterday and years
more than Egyptian, men at their greatest and men
at their oddest, with additions from faëry and fable,
jostle in Emerson's pages, a parti-coloured multi-
lingual temple-crowd, the figures and voices which
have kept the world interesting. Something of the
same pleasure may be had from Plutarch, one of
Emerson's favourite authors, but not in equal degree.
Both writers have that large and generous temper
which the study of biography promotes. "We owe to
biography," says Emerson, "the fortification of our
hope." We owe to it also the widening of our charity.

He knew the world, of course, largely at second-
hand — as Shakespeare knew kings by gaping at
them, Italy by having a summer in his private heart;
as Trollope knew the souls of bishops and archdeacons
out of nothing more intimate than their gaiters. It is
the privilege of genius to be thus second-hand; and
only so does it find leisure for inspiration. Emerson
speaks often of "the superstition of travelling," as he
calls it. Let a man go home; *in* him is the universe.
For the remote life that he elected for himself he has
made an eloquent and ungainsayable plea in the last
words of the last of his *Lectures for the Times*. Since
I do not know whether we are less material in our
civilisation than we were then, or less need voices to

speak to us about interests "not marketable or perishable," I will leave with you his plea for the scholar, the idealist: I could pick no passage which better illustrates his eloquence:

Amidst the downward tendency and proneness of things, when every voice is raised for a new road or another statute, or a subscription of stock, for an improvement in dress, or in dentistry, for a new house, or a larger business, for a political party or the division of an estate — will you not suffer one or two solitary voices in the land speaking for thoughts and principles not marketable or perishable? Soon these improvements and mechanical inventions will be superseded; these modes of living lost out of memory; these cities rotted, ruined by war, by new seats of trade, or the geologic changes: — all gone, like the shells which sprinkle the sea-beach with a white colony today, for ever renewed to be for ever destroyed. But the thoughts which these few hermits strove to proclaim by silence, as well as by speech, not only by what they did, but by what they forbore to do, shall abide in beauty and strength, to reorganize themselves in nature, to invest themselves anew in other, perhaps higher-endowed and happier-mixed clay than ours, in fuller union with the surrounding system.

✿✿✿✿✿✿✿✿✿✿✿✿✿✿✿✿✿✿✿✿✿✿✿✿✿

CLOUGH

IT IS not in my mind to claim for Clough a place
among the great poets. But it is not in my heart,
having spoken of Matthew Arnold and of Emerson, to
let Clough go by, as though he were interesting on the
account of others, as though he were respectable by
his connexions, but in himself negligible. I could not
but feel kindly towards him in any case; for he was
the first, so far as I know, of a band of adventurers
since numerous — so numerous that their courage no
longer catches the eye; he was the first fellow of an
Oxford college to come and teach here in Cambridge.
He was brought here by Emerson. Emerson had been
his guest in Oxford four years before. Together he
and Emerson had watched in Paris the Revolution of
'48. But there were other reasons why Clough should
come here. He had only just missed being born an
American citizen. He had the bad luck to be born in
Liverpool; but his childhood, up to his tenth year,
had been passed in the United States.[1] To that early
experience he perhaps owed a characteristic which,
among his own countrymen, exposed him to friendly
ridicule; he had an intense love of liberty. In one of
his first letters from Cambridge this love of liberty
shines with a subdued light. "Drink," he writes, "in

[1] His parents lived in Charleston, South Carolina. Clough's brother,
George Augustus Clough, is buried in the cemetery of St. Michael's
Church, Charleston (near the Broad Street Gate). The tombstone is

the shape of wine or spirits is actually forbidden. Temperance is established by law. . . . This is said to be of great benefit in the country places." The last clause suggests that in the cities, in Cambridge and Boston, the benefits were either less or less obvious. Freedom has its paradoxes; but Clough was not the man to be depressed by them. If his drinks were not free, his lectures were. The Harvard Faculty invited him to lecture; but they did not pay him for doing so. For some time Clough took pupils; or the pupils took Clough. I think that they did not particularly like him. He taught them ethics, he tells us; throughout life he had a strong taste for making men morally better — he had not been a pupil of the great Dr. Arnold for nothing. I fancy that Emerson, whose métier was hopefulness, had a little miscalculated his ability to find Clough employment. Clough tried writing for the press; one or two of the better American journals printed essays for him that were good,

inscribed with some verses written by Clough, which have not, I think, been published:

> Of all thy kindred at thy dying day
> Were none to speed thee on thy solemn way;
> Yet ever lives distinct and deeply dear
> Their sight with them of this thy corner here;
> Each heart so oft hath come and sought and seen
> That ocean space hath shrunk to naught between,
> And more their own seems now the stranger's shore
> Than when with thee they dwelt on it before.

Clough, during his residence in Cambridge, lodged in a house on Appian Way, which stood on the site now occupied by the new buildings of Radcliffe College. The house, a small but charming frame building, was saved from destruction by Mr. and Mrs. Hull, who removed it entire to Coolidge Road and now live in it.

without being good journalism. Emerson tried to puff his poetry in a review. But puff as he might, Emerson was a man unable to emit any but true breath. The review is still extant; but it is easier, reading it, to think Emerson a sincere man than to suppose Clough a great poet. However, of the book reviewed, "a whole edition," writes Clough, "was printed *and sold*, they say, in Cambridge." Emerson put Clough to translating Plutarch. Plutarch was Emerson's favourite author. But he was not the favourite author of all the world; and though Clough completed some portion of his task, it was one not likely to put money in his purse. For Emerson, Clough retained throughout life a very deep veneration. "I more and more," he says, "recognise his superiority to everybody I have seen." Of his sojourn in Cambridge, though it did not bring him the advantages which he had hoped, he kept always a grateful memory. The ladies of Boston — may I add? — caused him uneasiness. They all seemed out of health. This impairment of health Clough traces to "the endless trouble" which they took "keeping servants doing things properly and nicely."

Clough had, in fact, good reason at all times to feel kindly towards America. What Charles Eliot Norton has said about Clough's first book, the *Bothie*, is true, I think, of all his work: "Its merit was more deeply felt and more generously acknowledged by American than by English readers." The *Bothie* was printed in America shortly after its first appearance in England, nearly four years before Clough came to Cambridge.

Clough's other long poem, the *Amours de Voyage*,
appeared first in America, and was, indeed, never
published in England during his lifetime. His American publishers paid him for it "a very handsome
sum" — the only money, he says, that he ever received for verse-making. It was an American firm,
again, which published his Plutarch: England, he told
Norton, "thinks Plutarch an old fool." The first col-
lected edition of his poems appeared in one and the
same year (the year following his death) in England
and America. Here were printed some of the *Mari
Magno* tales, upon which he had been engaged in the
last years of his life. They occupied the leisure of his
voyage to Greece and Constantinople; but they commemorate, in fact, his voyage to America nine years
previously; one of the characters in the prologue is a
portrait of James Russell Lowell.

Lowell, in 1871, uttered concerning Clough a proph-
ecy, of which the phrases are well known: "Clough
will be thought a hundred years hence," he wrote,
"to have been the truest expression in verse of the
moral and intellectual tendencies, the doubt and
struggle towards settled conviction, of the period in
which he lived." It will take the best part still of half
a century to refute that completely. If it should happen not to be refuted, I should think Clough — what
he never was in life — lucky; and Lowell lucky too.
No doubt, those parts of Clough's poetry which
Lowell may be supposed especially to have in mind
are, and will continue to be, significant documents in
the history of the Victorian spirit. But, if I may say

what I really think — and I see no reason why I should not — they present a phase of that spirit which is likely more and more to lose interest. A hundred years hence — for, with Lowell, I like to put a respectable interval between the flash of prediction and the thunderous mutter of contradiction — a hundred years hence, it will surprise me if the nice distinctions of religious belief which troubled men like Clough retain much more than a pathological interest. A hundred years hence the comment made upon them by Emerson a hundred years ago will seem truer for the passage of time: "As men's prayers are a disease of the will, so are their creeds a disease of the intellect."

I do not mean, when I say that, to dismiss as not worth reading all that section of Clough's poetry which he dedicates to religious reflection. Nor do I intend malice if I hazard the conjecture that, in this section, his best power lies in satire. I say *lies* in satire, rather than shews itself in satire; for Clough was unwilling, I fancy, to exploit fully, to mine deeply, the vein of satire in himself. Yet in satire was to be sought, perhaps, the proper artistic outlet for his self-torturing disposition. The popular judgment which has made *The Latest Decalogue* one of the few poems of Clough which is widely known obeys, I think, a true instinct. But I regret greatly the wrong direction which I feel to have been given to the study of Clough's poetry by the emphasis placed on those parts of it which express his struggle towards religious conviction. One or two of his religious poems will

always be read, perhaps, with interest — *Easter Day*
for example, and the fragment entitled *The Shadow*:

> Eat, drink, and die, for we are souls bereaved:
>   Of all the creatures under heaven's wide cope
>   We are most hopeless, who had once most hope,
> And most beliefless, who had most believed . . .
>
> And, oh, good men of ages yet to be,
> Who shall believe *because* ye did not see —
>   Oh, be ye warned, be wise!
>   No more with pleading eyes,
>   And sobs of strong desire,
>   Unto the empty vacant void aspire,
> Seeking another and impossible birth
> That is not of your own, and only, mother, earth.
> But if there is no other life for you,
> Sit down and be content, since this must even do.

That is from the first Part of *Easter Day*; and it has,
I think, its own emotional quality. But it keeps
us in the region of negatives; and no one felt more
deeply than Clough himself that art is some kind of
affirmation:

> O Thou that in our bosom's shrine
> Dost dwell, unknown because divine,
> I thought to speak, I thought to say,
> "The light is here," "behold the way,"
> "The voice was thus," and "thus the word,"
> And "this I saw," and "that I heard," —
> But from the lips that half essayed
> The imperfect utterance fell unmade

— utterance imperfect, from the point of view not
merely of peace of mind, but of art. Once only, I
think, in his *Religious Poems*, does Clough win to
perfect utterance:

O only Source of all our light and life,
   Whom as our truth, our strength, we see and feel,
But whom the hours of mortal moral strife
   Alone aright reveal!

Mine inmost soul, before Thee inly brought,
   Thy presence owns ineffable, divine;
Chastised each rebel self-encentered thought,
   My will adoreth Thine.

With eye down-dropt, if then this earthly mind
   Speechless remain, or speechless e'en depart;
Nor seek to see — for what of earthly kind
   Can see Thee as Thou art? —

If well-assured 'tis but profanely bold
   In thought's abstractest forms to seem to see,
It dare not dare the dread communion hold
   In ways unworthy Thee,

O not unowned, Thou shalt unnamed forgive,
   In worldly walks the prayerless heart prepare;
And if its work in life it seems to live,
   Shalt make that work be prayer.

Nor times shall lack, when while the work it plies,
   Unsummoned powers the blinding film shall part,
And scarce by happy tears made dim, the eyes
   In recognition start.

But, as Thou willest, give or e'en forbear
   The beatific supersensual sight,
So, with Thy blessing blest, that humbler prayer
   Approach Thee morn and night.

That is taken from the volume entitled *Ambarvalia*.
It cannot be too often said that most of those poems
of Clough which are distinctively religious in character were not published by himself. This one was;
and I think it closes a period in him. *Ambarvalia*
(what unlucky titles, what *unselling* titles, Clough

always managed to find for his books!), *Ambarvalia*
was published in 1849. It contains, we know from the
author's statement, poems composed at different
times during the ten-year period 1839–49. It may
be called, therefore, Clough's first book; though, in
date of actual publication, *The Bothie of Tober-na-
Fuosich* has priority by a whole year. The *Bothie* appeared just after Clough, under pressure of religious
scruples, had resigned his Oxford tutorship. His
friends were expecting from him some sort of a religious apologia. "In later days," says his wife, "he
would often speak with amusement of the disappoint-
ment which the appearance of these lively verses
produced among those who looked for a serious vindi-
cation of his conduct." Whether *Ambarvalia* was
meant to afford some sort of salve to this disappoint-
ment, I do not know. But with the poem which I
have just quoted, with *Qui Laborat Orat*, Clough had
at least found expression for the creed by which here-
after he was to live. I cannot feel that *Ambarvalia* deserves the praise which, for example, Palgrave has
given to it, who ranks some of its pieces with the best
of Tennyson and Browning. On the same level as
Qui Laborat Orat I should put only one other piece —
that entitled, in the later editions, "A Protest." It is a
poem still not so well known as it should be; and that
must excuse me for quoting the whole of it:

> Light words they were, and lightly, falsely said:
> She heard them, and she started, — and she rose,
> As in the act to speak: the sudden thought
> And unconsidered impulse led her on.

In act to speak she rose, but with the sense
Of all the eyes of that mixed company
Now suddenly turned upon her, some with age
Hardened and dulled, some cold and critical;
Some in whom vapours of their own conceit,
As moist malarious mists the heavenly stars,
Still blotted out their good, the best at best
By frivolous laugh and prate conventional
All too untuned for all she thought to say —
With such a thought the mantling blood to her cheek
Flushed-up, and o'er-flushed itself, blank night her soul
Made dark, and in her all her purpose swooned.
She stood as if for sinking.   Yet anon
With recollections clear, august, sublime,
Of God's great truth, and right immutable,
Which, as obedient vassals, to her mind
Came summoned of her will, in self-negation
Quelling her troublous earthy consciousness,
She queened it o'er her weakness.   At the spell
Back rolled the ruddy tide, and leaves her cheek
Paler than erst, and yet not ebbs so far
But that one pulse of one indignant thought
Might hurry it hither in flood.   So as she stood
She spoke.   God in her spoke and made her heard.

On the same height with the two pieces which I
have quoted some persons would place the lines be
ginning "As ships becalmed . . ." It is a poem which
has charm and pathos; and its figure of the separated
ships, its parable of broken friendship, enshrines a
personal experience. The head of an Oxford college
told me once how he was discussing the poem with
another person, whose name he did not give, who
broke off the conversation — "For you know," he
said, "I was the other ship, the lost friend."

I come back to the "lively verses," as Mrs. Clough
properly calls them, of the *Bothie*. Clough's English

friends were always wanting the wrong thing from him; and this lively poem disappointed them. What business has a man to be lively when he has just sacrificed his livelihood to a religious punctilio? And what business had a man to write hexameters?

I am not going to argue the pros and cons of this, or any other, kind of English hexameters. Yet the metre, I may notice, if it did not help the poem with English readers, certainly had a good deal to do with its vogue in America. Clough, in a letter to Emerson, bids him tell Longfellow that "it was a reading aloud of his *Evangeline* . . ., which coming after a reperusal of the 'Iliad' occasioned this outbreak of hexameters." Even so, we must not remember Longfellow and forget Homer; for not only does some of the diction of the *Bothie* come home, as Matthew Arnold rightly said, "with the true Homeric ring," but the temper of the poem has Homeric freshness. The outstanding merits of the poem have nowhere been better put than in some sentences of Charles Eliot Norton, which, from this Chair, I need no excuse for quoting: "The fact," writes Norton,[1] "that its essential form and local colouring were purely and genuinely English, and that this gratified the curiosity felt in this country concerning the social habits and ways of life in the mother land, while on the other hand its spirit was in sympathy with the most liberal and progressive thought of the age, may sufficiently account for its popularity here. But the lovers of poetry found delight in it apart from these char-

[1] *Poems of Arthur Hugh Clough*, Boston, 1862, pp. xix–xx.

acteristics — in its fresh descriptions of Nature, its
healthy manliness of tone, its scholarly construction,
its lively humour, its large thought, quickened and
deepened by the imagination of the poet."

One thing only Norton forgets to say — Clough has
a fine gift for telling a story. I am not sure that it is
not, of all his gifts, the best. He would be more read
today than he is but that we seem to have lost the old
human liking for a story, above all for a simple one;
nor today am I sure that a story the more commends
itself to us for carrying, what Norton rightly empha-
sises in Clough, a "healthy manliness of tone."
Clough's story is laid in one of the most beautiful regions of Scotland; nearly thirty years ago I read it in
its setting of mountain and lake; and again but three
years ago in the same setting. On the latter occasion,
I found in that part of Scotland at least as many
Americans as English. Some of them, — may I suggest? — might do worse, on their next trip, than take
with them Clough's *Bothie*. Incidentally, it illustrates a feature of English University life which is, I
am told, strange to American habits — the vacation
reading-party in which professor and pupil mix
on the assumption that the pupil is a grown man
and that the professor has still something of the boy
in him.

In the year in which he published this story,
Clough wrote yet another and, I think, a still better
story, yet again in his characteristic hexameters; the
Amours de Voyage. Here you may discover plainly,
what already you suspect from the *Bothie*, that his

real field is, not as you had supposed, religious moping
— I use that phrase as being conveniently compen-
dious; it needs qualifying, of course — but the
comedy of manners. It had to wait nine years for a
publisher. But it was written in 1849. Clough and
Emerson, I have said, had watched together in Paris
the tragi-comedy of '48. Clough had gone on to
Rome, where he was the spectator of yet another
political tragi-comedy. The *Amours de Voyage* paints
vigorously some of the scenes of the siege of Rome;
and gives interesting expression to the feelings excited by the political events of the time in the mind
of an Englishman who still thought of freedom somewhat like an American. I said I was not going to
argue about hexameters. Mr. Whibley has amused
himself by printing some of the hexameters of this
poem as though they were prose:

And now the crowd is coming, has turned, has crossed
that last barricade, is here at my side. In the middle they
drag at something. What is 't? Ha! bare swords in the air,
held up? There seem to be voices pleading and hands
putting back; official, perhaps; but the swords are many,
and bare in the air . . . on that evening . . . three, or four,
or, it may be, five, of these people were slaughtered.

"There is merit in the writing," Mr. Whibley says,
truly, "merit of colour and rapidity. But Clough is
fighting a hopeless battle against the genius of the
language." I will not argue it; I agree with Mr.
Whibley about the "merit in the writing"; it has
something, indeed, of the merit of a paragraph of
Carlyle's *French Revolution*. Clough can paint a living

scene. But he can also write hexameters which are both metre and poetry. Here are some [1] —

Whither depart the souls of the brave who die in battle,
Die in the last lost fight, for the cause that perishes with them?
Are they upborne from the field on the slumberous pinions of
    angels
Unto a far-off home, where the weary rest from their labour,
And the deep wounds are healed, and the bitter and burning
    moisture
Wiped from the generous eyes? or do they linger, unhappy,
Pining and haunting the grave of their by-gone hope and en-
    deavour?

However, I want to commend the *Amours de Voyage* to you *as a story*. It is a love-story, well told, and with a fine quality of characterisation. It is a love-story which comes to nothing. It cannot be said to end unhappily; but it ends singularly true to life, nobody marrying anybody; not that that always happens in life — it would be hard to keep life going, if it did — but it so often happens that it is interesting to meet it in poetry. Emerson, of whom in general I find it hard to speak ill, behaved stupidly about it; for it is stupid, to miss the whole point of the story; and that is what he does. He pressed Clough to rewrite the latter part, to give it a happy ending. The theme of lovers' preliminaries protracted till the story dies in the preparation of itself had always a fascination for Clough; he liked a hero who could not bring his resolution to the sticking-point of committing marriage, and who went away not much the worse for not hav-

[1] The fifth line substitutes, in its first foot, an anapaest for a dactyl, and is none the worse for doing so, unless we read it as though it did not.

ing what he wanted. He uses the theme again in
Mari Magno.

I suppose that *Mari Magno* cannot be called
Clough's masterpiece. If that is so, it is only because
he died in the middle of writing it. Even the best
parts of it shew traces of hurried and unrevised composition, stop-gap phrases and stop-gap lines, words
wrongly placed or falsely emphasised, individual sentiments not braced to effectiveness, descriptions that
straggle. I believe the book is very little read. Yet
nothing that Clough wrote gives me the same sense of
being in contact with a nature genuinely poetical. I
have said that I did not wish to claim for him a place
among the great poets; but at least *Mari Magno* per-
suades me that such a place would have been his if he
had had longer life. It has been debated whether, in
these Tales told on shipboard, he was trying to catch
the manner of Chaucer, or whether the style of them
is studied upon Crabbe. But the question ought
never to have been raised. In his last years he read
both these poets with keen pleasure. Of Crabbe, he
writes: "There is no one more purely English in the
Dutch manner." "Sometimes," he adds, "though
rarely, he has really the highest merit." What it is to
be "purely English, in the Dutch manner" I am not
too sure; but I am sure that it is not one of the effects
at which Clough aims in *Mari Magno*. That the Tales
should look off to those of Chaucer was to be expected.
After all, they are Tales; and in the history of English
poetry who is there that can tell a Tale except Chaucer? But in fact the merit of Clough, in these Tales,

is, not that he is like Chaucer — though that would
be, certainly, a very signal merit — but that he is like
himself. His manner is individual; and so much do
I feel this that only Chaucer himself and Wordsworth, I am inclined to say, are equally individual
with the same absence of artifice. It is not difficult
to be individual in a manner strained or complicated,
in the manner, say, of Donne or of Browning. But
the plain style has no resources other than those of
character.

To speak so is to praise Clough highly. But if I
seem to praise these Tales beyond their merit, at least
what I can say can be checked; there is nothing that
I more desire than that someone who has not read
Mari Magno should be lured into doing so. Let him
begin at the beginning. Not all the Tales are equally
good. But the two first are, by good luck, the best.
There is some want of verbal art in them, I have said
already; but they shew an art of feeling so perfect
that it requires almost a bad nature to miss it. This
art has, for its governing characters, the two qualities
which Palgrave remarked as pre-eminently distinguishing Clough as a man — tenderness and noble-
ness. The two middle Tales — there are six Tales in
all — are somewhat slight and confused — they are
those, perhaps, in which Clough is most like Chaucer
and least like himself. The fifth Tale, the Clergyman's
Second Tale, if it is not as good as his first, has more
of a story; and the story is well told, the manner of it
admirably adapted to the character of the narrator;
and the brief comments upon it of the listeners are

excellent. The book ends with the Second Tale of the Lawyer: another good Tale, the narrative being, perhaps, more lively, and even dramatic, than that used elsewhere. It must be conceded, however, that neither of the Lawyer's Tales, nor the Lawyer's manner of telling them, are particularly well adjusted to his profession. He is said to have been drawn from Thackeray; but he seems to me redolent of Rugby and Balliol. Not one of the Tales, let me add, could possibly have been written by anyone but an Englishman; the two last will be thought by some persons too much to reflect the narrow morality of the Victorians; both are old-fashioned tales. Yet any morality, I have sometimes thought, is better than none. Clough went a little further than that; he did not like his ethics too good-natured. He hated easy going; and he tended to count no one happy whom nature had not touched with a hand "too noble to be kind":

> O for some winnowing wind, to the empty air
> This chaff of easy sympathies to bear
> Far off, and leave me of myself aware!
> While thus this over-health deludes me still,
> So willing that I know not what I will;
> O for some friend, or more than friend, austere,
> To make me know myself, and make me fear!
> O for some touch, too noble to be kind,
> To awake to life the mind within the mind!

The last of Clough's poems to be published — like *Mari Magno*, unfinished and unrevised — was the satirical drama, or dialogue, *Dipsychus*. It had been written in Venice in 1850. When he wrote it Clough was clearly fresh from the reading of Goethe's *Faust*;

fresh, again, I do not doubt, from reading *Don Juan*
— carried to *Don Juan*, of course, by the associations
which link Byron and Venice. The best parts of the
poem are those in which Clough yields himself, not
merely to satire, but to irresponsible satire. The hero
is a religious moper, the author of *Easter Day;* but he
is attended always by a mocking spirit, the author of
The Latest Decalogue. The moper and the mocker,
Mephistopheles and the Muff, Dullness and the
Devil — these are the two souls in one person to
which the poem owes its title. All along the line the
Devil has the best of the argument, and the sympathy of the reader; not because he is the Devil, and
his antagonist a dull dog, but because he is a first-class
literary performer. When the Devil is off the stage,
the piece drags — the blank-verse monologues of the
Muff are mostly wearisome. But the Devil, save for
one scene in which he catches from his opponent the
trick of unrhyming monologue, the Devil of *Dipsychus* is — after Butler and Byron — the best satirist
our literature can shew in that order of satiric verse
of which *Hudibras* and *Don Juan* are the supreme
examples. It is a reproach to our criticism that a
satire so gay and so going should be so little read.
The truth is that nearly all Clough's readers have
been of the wrong sort; they have been dull persons —
clergymen with doubts, and theologically minded
laymen — and they have liked only Clough's dull
parts. I wish that I had left myself time to speak the
proper praise of this brilliant fragment. Apart from
the astonishing cleverness of its satire, and its fine

courage of bad rhymes, it has a poetical merit which it shares with the *Amours de Voyage* — it has caught the colour of the Italian scene. Even from the dull parts of it I do not always find it easy to withhold my sympathy. The nervous preoccupation which the poem shews with the subject of moral purity I cannot think indicative of perfect poetical health. The victory of Mephistopheles over the Muff is a sheer triumph of cleverness; and I think that I enjoy it more than Clough meant me to do. The moral disaster of Dipsychus himself leaves me a little uninterested. Yet I cannot find it in my heart to call dull either the temper or the style of lines like these:

> Ah! me, me!
> Clear stars above, thou roseate westward sky,
> Take up my being into yours; assume
> My sense to know you only; steep my brain
> In your essential purity; or, great Alps,
> That wrapping round your heads in solemn clouds
> Seem sternly to sweep past our vanities,
> Lead me with you — take me away, preserve me!
>
> O moon and stars, forgive! and thou, clear heaven,
> Look pureness back into me.   Oh, great God!
> Why, why, in wisdom and in grace's name,
> And in the name of saints and saintly thoughts,
> Of mothers, and of sisters, and chaste wives,
> And angel woman-faces we have seen,
> And angel woman-spirits we have guessed,
> And innocent sweet children, and pure love,
> Why did I ever one brief moment's space
> But parley with this filthy Belial?

I suppose that is all very Victorian. Yet perhaps in our weaker moments — which are sometimes our better ones — we are all of us more Victorian than we care to allow.

America — and Cambridge — have, I have said, a rather special responsibility for Clough. He was an American discovery, a Cambridge find. It belongs to the American temper, I sometimes fancy, to be the first to find great writers — and the first to find them out. I think you have forgotten Clough too quickly. There is a good deal of him which I think deserves rediscovering. For myself, I first read him five-and-thirty years ago, from a greedy theological appetite. I liked his questioning spirit, for I was at an age when religious doubt is as sweet as first love. Today, I do not ask that anybody should rediscover Clough's religious poetry. Far rather, it is litter that I want to see cleared away — or the greater part of it is litter. But it hides work worth salving — work of a positive quality. It is odd how often the good of poets and of men gets buried under theology.

❖❖❖❖❖❖❖❖❖❖❖❖❖❖❖❖❖❖❖❖❖❖❖❖❖

THE TESTAMENT OF BEAUTY [1]

I DO NOT know how old Homer was when he wrote
the Odyssey. Longinus' comment upon it is well
known. "I speak of old age," he says, "but it is none
the less the old age of Homer." The Odyssey, he
means, is not so great a poem as the Iliad: as an old
man's work tends to be, it is in parts a little garru-
lous. But it is still Homer. Mr. Robert Bridges published his *Testament of Beauty* on the day on which he
entered his eighty-sixth year. Yet a good critic,
whose name I think I can guess, has said of it already
that it is not only his greatest poem, but his youngest.
If that be true, or if anything like it be true, then the
history of literature can scarcely afford a parallel; but,
for a like achievement, we shall have to go to the
sister art of music, to the old age of Verdi. That from
that art we should have to seek our analogue would,
I think, especially please Mr. Bridges; who, like Milton, it may be suspected, has sometimes not known,
of that "blest pair of Sirens," Music and Poetry,
which the more truly held his heart; and who perhaps laboured no lines of this, his last poem, more
lovingly than those in which he speaks of the violin:

> even as those well-toned viols, matured by time, which once,
> when the Muse visited Italy to prepare
> a voice of beauty for the joy of her children,

[1] When this lecture was delivered, Mr. Bridges was still living.

wer fashioned by Amati and Stradivari and still,
treasured in their mellow shapeliness, fulfil
the genius of her omnipotent destiny, —
speaking with incantation of strange magic to charm
the dreams that yet undreamt lurk in the unfathom'd deep
of mind, unfeatured hopes and dim desires,
uttermost forms of all things that shall be.

For my own part, I feel not too much disposed to ask whether, in *The Testament of Beauty*, Mr. Bridges is in fact greater than himself, nor whether the poem has all that abundant youth that is alleged. In our first surprise, we are likely to exaggerate its youthfulness; and I do not know that to do so is to pay Mr. Bridges a compliment. After all, what does life mean if, at eighty-five, a man has still the heart, or the want of it, not to be as old as he is? We must not allow some of the modernities of the poem too much to engage our judgment. Airplanes, wireless, the latest discoveries in Mesopotamia, the newest types of agricultural machinery, the post-war undergraduate, Freudism and a whole book upon the subject of sex — all these things remind us that Mr. Bridges knows in what order of world he has grown old. And certainly we may felicitate him that he should retain into extreme age all that lively interest which he has in the modern world, its inventions and curiosities, and that he should bring to all these things a free speculative spirit. Nor will anybody grudge him what I may call his occasional youthful clevernesses — as when, speaking of the assimilation of European science by the Oriental peoples, their magi, he says, their wise

men, "hav seen the electric light in the West"; or
when, commenting on the displacement of the scythe
by the reaping-machine, and speculating what the
small creatures in the corn make of it, surely, he says,
"the grasshopper wondering knoweth his god."
These pleasant sophomorisms no one would wish
away. Again, when he touches questions of politics,
I do not know how young Mr. Bridges is not prepared to be. In his contempt for the mob he is as
young as Shakespeare — and as delightfully unrea-
sonable. Indeed, this poem would not be Mr.
Bridges' if whim and prejudice nowhere shewed their
forehead — or even their teeth.

None the less, it becomes us, reading it, to remember that the book is, what its title proclaims it, a
testament. It is the final deliverance, the last will
and monition, upon the subject of beauty, of a lifelong student of the beautiful. The writer of it, making his last dispositions, is in the nature of things
uninfluenced by the ordinary literary motives, vanity
and love of glory. But he wishes before he takes
leave of the sensible world to put upon record his
experience of the beautiful, what it has meant in his
life, what he conceives to be its relation to truth,
what promise he finds in it of immortality for man's
spirit. Mr. Bridges' title, let me say here, is in itself a
fine stroke of talent. The end of Gower's never-end-
ing *Confessio Amantis* relates how Venus directed its
author to seek out Chaucer and, in the name of the
Queen of Love, bid him crown his life-work by writing a "testament of love":

> And gret wel Chaucer whan ye mete,
> As mi disciple and mi poete . . .
> Forthi now in hise daies olde
> Thow shalt him telle this message,
> That he upon his later age,
> To sette an ende of alle his werk,
> As he which is myn owne clerk,
> Do make his testament of love . . .

Mr. Bridges, we may suppose, either knew those lines, or he knew the still extant *Testament of Love*, a dull prose treatise once attributed to Chaucer, but now known to have been written by one of his contemporaries, Thomas Usk.[1]

The title prepares us for a poem of which much of the quality is essentially Chaucerian. Nor is it for nothing that twice, in the body of his poem, Mr. Bridges has employed towards Chaucer that fashion of compliment which Virgil employed towards Ennius and others: twice he has rounded off a paragraph with a tag of Chaucerian verse —

> So priketh hem Nature in hir corages . . .
> And here I wol nat han to do of swich matere . . .

We may suppose again that his preoccupation with Chaucer dictated to Mr. Bridges some of his pleasant archaisms — birdes, Goddes, and the like. The diction generally owes, I should say, not a little to the father of all sweet and pure English; and I feel the same to be true of the manner and temper of the poem. If the manner of the poem is sometimes grave and Dan-

---

[1] Mr. Bridges uses the word *breed* in the sense of *sex*. Is it mere accident that it is so used already by Usk?

tesque, it is best, I think, where that manner gives place to one more domestic. If I had to name that quality in *The Testament of Beauty* which gives to it its true distinction, I should be disposed to say that it resided in a certain sweet and gentle seriousness. That I feel to be its proper praise; a truer praise than to impute to it any miracle of youth. It may be suspected, indeed, that Chaucer made especial appeal to Mr. Bridges just because, almost alone of our poets, Chaucer has, without the miracle of youth, achieved the miracle of poetry. If Mr. Bridges is like Chaucer in his sweet and gentle seriousness, he is like him also in a quality which may be thought rather more equivocal. He has — or he seems to me to have — both in reflection and in argumentation, something of Chaucer's naïveté. Of Aristotle and of the schoolmen, and of philosophers and scientists generally, what he says is often Chaucer-like — and child-like — in its simplicity. I do not know, let me add, where outside Chaucer we shall light upon any other poetry so essentially *English* in its temper.

The metre of the poem will be a stumbling-block to a good many persons. Already an American critic has speculated whether just this will not before long relegate the book to a place among "the curiosities of literature." I comfort myself that Chaucer took the same chance when, in the *Legend of Good Women* — which some scholars have supposed to be his *Testament of Love* — he used for the first time the heroic couplet, now the most familiar of all measures. I will say frankly, however, that it would not surprise me if over a good many generations *The Testament of Beauty* were read as a kind of dignified prose — or as we read Greek lyric. Somewhat so for centuries was Chaucer read; yet the fact that he could not scan Chaucer did not obscure for Dryden Chaucer's poetical greatness. That the unresting spirit of experimentation should have led Mr. Bridges to invent in his eighties a new metre is certainly astonishing. Yet, once again, I am not disposed to acclaim here any miracle of youthfulness. This new metre is not a dance measure. The feet of it have a slow, reflective, even dragging, character. It cannot be thought a particularly active metre — I think I could guess, if I did not know, to what years it belongs. Nor does Mr. Bridges pretend to have perfected his new instrument. It is not, I think, from mock modesty that he calls his verses "loose Alexandrines." For myself, I do not like them the less from the circumstance that they are a good deal wilful; that Mr. Bridges has withheld from them the deeper pains of art. In no other poem has he brought so little study to his metre. And this unstudied manner communicates itself, beyond the metre, to the composition as a whole. I cannot help wondering whether just this may not be accountable for the remarkable vogue which this poem has achieved. Whether Mr. Bridges has written greater poetry in the past I will, as I said, not ask. But if he has, the public has not found it out. Never before has he written a poem which was, as this has been, a great and immediate publishing success. This is his first *best-seller*; and the

reason for it may very well be that in this poem for
the first time he has, as we say, "let himself go";
that he has put more of nature, and less of art, into it
than into any other of his compositions.

A philosophical poem in four books: so, I suppose,
the book should properly be described. I cannot even
say that the philosophy is warranted not to bite; or
that it is as easy to keep out of the way of it as a man
might wish. I know how to read the *Georgics* of Virgil, leaving to the market-gardener and the veterin-
ary surgeon the things that are theirs, and enjoying
the digressions. I am skilled, reading Lucretius, to
dodge the atoms, swerve they never so unpredictably,
and hold the skirts of *dia Voluptas*. But *The Testament of Beauty* does not make easy skipping. The
reader must square his account to being argued with;
sometimes in good round terms, but quite often in
terms bad and angular. As against some other poets
who have been committed by their subject to the
jargon of philosophy, or the *plusquam* jargon of
science, it may be said for Mr. Bridges that he can
grin at his own grotesque:

> So that whether it be starch, oil, sugar, or alcohol
> 'tis ever our old customers, carbon and hydrogen,
> pirouetting with oxygen in their morris antics;
> the chemist booketh all of them as C H O.
> and his art is as mine, when I but figurate
> the twin persistent semitones of my Grand Chant . . .

That at least is in the right spirit — if I called it the
"poetry-go-hand" spirit, I do not suppose that Mr.
Bridges would make a heavy quarrel with me. It is

refreshing when from time to time poets put off their long faces. Or take again this:

Plato was pleased to launch his whole Utopia safely in absolute dreamland; but poor Socrates, on whom he fathered it, was left *in nubibus*, where Aristophanes in good jest had set him some twenty years afore; and our sophists, who lack claim to any shred of great Plato's glorious mantle of wisdom, have secured a good lien on his bluff. . . .

That kind of prose you will only take, of course, from a poet. In any case, before you refuse it, compare it with some of the prose of Wordsworth's *Excursion*, or even of his *Prelude*. Mr. Bridges, when he writes prose, knows it, and enjoys it. The spirit of mischief is upon him. But who ever caught Wordsworth being mischievous?

Yet I mention the *Prelude* for a reason which should have restrained me from mixing, with my mention of it, malice. For in truth I esteem it of all poems in our language the most purely *original*. I am not sure that Mr. Bridges' poem is like any other poem that I know; but if it is, it is like the *Prelude*. Some qualities of it I have mentioned which are Chaucerian. The Chaucerisms are conscious and deliberate. But the affinity with Wordsworth goes deeper, because it is, I feel, not much meditated. If Mr. Bridges has put his heart to school with any one of the romantics, it is not with Wordsworth, but with Shelley. There are passages of *The Testament of Beauty* which glow as Shelley glows, and as Wordsworth does not glow. Even so, for anything at all like Mr. Bridges' poem we must go back, I feel, to the *Prelude*. This is a more

stract argument; it has a greater number of sticky
places. But it has the same kind of originality.
Again and again, reading it, I have been brought up
sharply against the sense of things seen and said in
just that *original* fashion of which Wordsworth is the
master.

It is not easy, I have said, to dodge the argument
of the poem. The main lines of it are easy enough to
follow.

> How the mind of man from inconscient existence
> cometh thru' the animal by growth of reasoning
> toward spiritual conscience,

that is Mr. Bridges' theme. In the treatment of it,
the first book is introductory, and nearly all of it is
pure poetry — perhaps of any immersion in philosophy the most delightful part is trying the water with
one's toe. Beginning from the origin and growth of
intellectual Wonder, the book explains the spiritual
as, in all its departments, a differentiation of the
natural, as the flower is a differentiation of the leaf;
the four sections into which the introduction is
divided furnish together a brief outline of the natural
history of what Mr. Bridges calls Wisdom. The two
books which follow deal with the two fundamental
human instincts; the self-assertive instinct, which Mr.
Bridges calls "Selfhood," and the instinct of sex,
which he mostly prefers to speak of as "Breed."
Book II traces the evolution of Selfhood into altruism,
the passion of benevolence, an evolution conditioned
naturally by the fact of "Motherhood." Book III

instructs us how Breed is by like natural process converted into spiritual love. The fourth book is concerned with Ethick — the origin of the idea of duty, the place of pleasure in the good life, disposition and education, the relation of Reason to the idea of Beauty and to the material of the senses generally.

If it is not easy to dodge the argument, neither is it easy for Mr. Bridges to dodge the question whether there ought to be one. But he does — it suffices for him to have written, against all odds, the only readable philosophical poem since Lucretius. I fancy that he thinks his argument better, abstractly, than it is, i. e., better than I think it; and newer than it is, i. e., not as old as the hills and the human heart.[1] But I am sure, in any case, that the best comment upon the whole of it is to be given in his own words:

> and the secret of a poem
> lieth in the intimate echo of the poet's life.

The power of the argument, I mean, consists in the manner in which it reflects an experience. The same is in some degree true, no doubt, of the *De Rerum Natura* — though the power of Lucretius derives mainly, perhaps, from his proselytising ardour (Mr. Bridges is not much concerned to proselytise). But argument is reason, and poetry is beauty; and when I have read these four books — and four times have I read them with close attention, reasoning as best I could, and submitting (not always with the best grace in the world) to be reasoned with — after all this reading and re-reading I have to confess that I still do

[1] What is new is Mr. Bridges' audacious eclecticism.

not know how Mr. Bridges relates Reason to Beauty. By Beauty, he says,

> by Beauty it is that we come at Wisdom,
> but not by Reason at Beauty.

Yet Reason, or reasoning, has a front place in this *Testament of Beauty*; and when I hope that Mr. Bridges is at length going to tell me why, he breaks off:

> here break I off, knowing the goal was not for me,
> the while I ran on telling of what cannot be told.

Of the things that cannot be told Mr. Bridges has managed, none the less, to tell some in a manner of which the deep and original power cannot, I persuade myself, be matched outside the very greatest poetry.

Not all the four books of this poem are, I think, of equal merit. The introductory book is, as I have said, almost all pure poetry. If I may pick passages from it (and this is a new poem, so that it is, perhaps, not impertinent to proffer this kind of guidance), I would say that the whole of the *exordium*, the first 336 lines, is as lofty an example of reflective and descriptive poetry as our literature can afford. From the last lines of the *exordium* I will allow myself to illustrate Mr. Bridges' power in pure natural description, exercised in a picture, first, of cloudland, and then of woodland:

> The sky's unresting cloudland, that with varying play
> sifteth the sunlight thru' its figured shades, that now
> stand in massiv range, cumulated stupendous
> mountainous snowbillowy up-piled in dazzling sheen,
> Now like sailing ships on a calm ocean drifting,
> Now scatter'd wispy waifs, that neath the eager blaze
> disperse in air; Or now parcelling the icy inane

highspredd in fine diaper of silver and mother-of-pearl
freaking the intense azure; Now scurrying close o'erhead,
wild ink-hued random racers that fling sheeted rain
gustily, and with garish bows laughing o'erarch the land:
Or, if the spirit of storm be abroad, huge molten glooms
mount on the horizon stealthily, and gathering as they climb
deep-freighted with live lightning, thunder and drenching flood
rebuff the winds, and with black-purpling terror impend
til they be driven away, when grave Night peacefully
clearing her heavenly rondure of its turbid veils
layeth bare the playthings of Creation's babyhood;
and the immortal fireballs of her uttermost space
twinkle like friendly rushlights on the countryside.
       Them soon the jealous Day o'errideth to display
Earth's green robe, which the sun fostereth for shelter and shower;
The dance of young trees that in a wild birch-spinney
toss to and fro the cluster of their flickering crests,
as rye curtseying in array to the breeze of May;
The ancestral trunks that mightily in the forest choirs
rear stedfast colonnade, or imperceptibly
sway in tall pinewoods to their whispering spires;
The woodland's alternating hues, the vaporous bloom
of the first blushings and tender flushings of spring;
The slumbrous foliage of high midsummer's wealth;
Rich Autumn's golden quittance, to the bankruptcy
of the black shapely skeletons standing in snow:
Or, in gay months of swelling pomp, the luxury
of leisur'd gardens teeming with affection'd thought;
the heartfelt secrecy of rustic nooks, and valleys
vocal with angelic rilling of rocky streams,
by rambling country-lanes, with hazel and thorn embower'd
woodbine, bryony and wild roses; the landscape lure
of rural England, that held glory in native art
untill our painters took their new fashion from France.

We speak somewhat too loosely of poets *painting*
nature — nine times out of ten we are describing
some other operation, a process in some other me-
dium; for example, I am not prepared to say of

Wordsworth that he ever *paints* nature. But the
passage I have just read to you *is* painting — so far
as one art can be another; painting essentially rich
and deep in quality.

The first book ends as nobly as it begins, but in a
different manner of description — the historical.
Again and again you will find yourself asking,
throughout this poem, whether Mr. Bridges is at his
greatest in his landscapes or in his pictures of history.

> Long had the homing bees plundered the thymy flanks
> of famed Hymettus harvesting their sweet honey:
> agelong the dancing waves had lapp'd the Aegean isles
> and promontories of the blue Ionian shore
> — where in her Mediterranean mirror gazing
> old Asia's dreamy face wrinkleth to a westward smile

— long had that been so before the flower of art found
its unpredicted perfection in Athens:

> As some perfected flower, Iris or Lily, is born
> patterning heavenly beauty, a pictur'd idea
> that hath no other expression for us, nor coud hav:
> for thatt which Lily or Iris tell cannot be told
> by poetry or by music in their secret tongues,
> nor is discerptible in logic, but is itself
> an absolute piece of Being, and we know not,
> nay, nor search not by what creativ miracle
> the soul's language is writ in perishable forms —
> yet are we aware of such existences crowding,
> mysterious beauties unexpanded, unreveal'd,
> phantasies intangible investing us closely,
> hid only from our eyes by skies that will not clear;
> activ presences, striving to force an entrance,
> like bodiless exiled souls in dumb urgence pleading
> to be brought to birth in our conscient existence,
> as if our troubled lot wer the life they long'd for;
> even as poor mortals thirst for immortality: —

And every divination of Natur or reach of Art
is nearer attainment to the divine plenitude
of understanding, and in moments of Vision
   their unseen company is the breath of Life: —

By such happy influence of their chosen goddess
the mind of Hellas blossom'd with a wondrous flow'r,
flaming in summer season, and in its autumn fall
ripening an everlasting fruit, that in dying
scatter'd its pregnant seeds into all the winds of heav'n:
nor ever again hath like bloom appear'd among men.

The second book conducts us into regions where we
are never for a moment safe from argument. Yet, if
I may say boldly what I think, this is, none the less,
the master book, gathering greatness through all the
stretch of it. You must bear to be vexed with talk
about the "autarchy" of "Selfhood," and the manner in which, by way of "Motherhood," Selfhood
transmutes itself into altruism — a process offering,
I should fancy, difficulties which a trained philosopher might think more considerable than they seem
to Mr. Bridges. But out of these vexations Mr.
Bridges redeems you without intolerable delay into
tracts of poetry where you are willing to take all his
answers for granted. Let me give you, at full length,
his picture of the self-assertive Youth of Man, going
forth into the world all-conquering: so long as Faith
attends him, all-conquering; but without Faith, without the assurance of things not seen, he makes head
for disaster:

And now full light of heart he hath willingly pass'd out
thru' the sword-gates of Eden into the world beyond:
He wil be child no more: in his revel of knowledge
all the world is his own: all the hope of mankind

is sharpen'd to a spearpoint in his bright confidence,
as he rideth forth to do battle, a Chevalier
in the joyous travail of the everlasting dawn:
There is nought to compare then, truly nought to compare:
and wer not Fortune fickle in her loving kindness,
all wer well with a man — for his life is at flower,
nor hath he any fear: πόθεν θανᾱτου νῦν
μνημονεύσειεν ἀν ἐν ἀκμῇ τοσαύτῃ?
But since her favor is inscrutable and uncertain,
and of her multiplicity she troubleth not
at the interaction of diverse self-consequences,
ther wil be blastings and blightings of hope and love,
and rude shocks that affray; yet to the enamour'd soul
evil is irrelevant and will be brush'd aside:
rather 'tis as with Art, wherein special beauty
springeth of obstacles that hav been overcome
and to graces transform'd; so the lover in life
will make obstructions serve, and from all resistance
gain strength: his reconcilement with suffering is eased
by fellow-suffering, and in pride of his calling
good warriorship welcometh the challenge of death.
    Beneath the spaceless dome of the soul's firmament
he liveth in the glow of a celestial fire,
fed by whose timeless beams our small obedient sun
is as a cast-off satellite, that borroweth
from the great Mover of all; and in the light of light
man's little works, strewn on the sands of time, sparkle
like cut jewels in the beatitude of God's countenance.
    But heav'nward tho' the chariot be already mounted,
'tis Faith alone can keep the charioteer in heart —
Nay, be he but irresolute the steeds wil rebel,
and if he looketh earthward they wil follow his gaze;
and ever as to earth he neareth, and vision cleareth
of all that he feareth, and the enemy appeareth
waving triumphant banners on the strongholds of ill,
his mirroring mind wil tarnish, and mortal despair
possess his soul: then surely Nature hath no night
dark as that black darkness that can be felt: no storm
blind as the fury of Man's self-destructiv passions,
no pestilence so poisonous as his hideous sins.

Parts of that, the penultimate paragraph especially, remind me of Shelley — I do not know where else to look for poetry of just that order, flaming and exalted in the same style.

The book ends with reflections upon the subject of war. Of the Great War it sums the cause in a memorable phrase — "mankind's crowded uncleanness of soul." We have heard young men upon the War, in plenty, and speaking with just title, God knows. Some of them have seen things, and others of them have seen visions. But there is a western front of man's nature where all is for ever disquiet; and Mr. Bridges surveys it unhappily, only here for his spiritual discouragements finding no palliative. His commentary upon it ends with a notable confession. On the day of Armistice, the War was ended. But what end had been made to that in which it began — "mankind's crowded uncleanness of soul"? On that day, my spirit, he says,

> was heavier within me, and felt a profounder fear
> than ever it knew in all War's darkest dismay.

In the first weeks of the War, it may be said here — for we forget everything too easily — the citizens of Oxford saw Mr. Bridges, already then over seventy, drilling daily in the Parks.

In the third book I seem to find some flagging of the mental powers, some tiring of the imagination itself: the wings of the spirit, hitherto strong and greatly adventurous, droop a little. Technicalities thicken, and cloud perception. The theme is the evolution of

sex; and the treatment of it is everywhere frank, in
some places naïve. The best pictures are the historical — of Dante, Shakespeare, Lucretius, there are
things nobly said, and Mr. Bridges has put a good
deal of his heart into an elaborated idyll of the Prov-
ence of the Troubadours:

> While in such play Count Raymond's folk lived joyfully,
> Provence seem'd to mankind the one land of delight, —
> a country where a man might fairly choose to dwell;
> tho' some would rather praise the green languorous isles,
> Hawaii or Samoa, and some the bright Azores,
> Kashmire the garden of Ind, or Syrian Lebanon
> and flowery Carmel; or wil vaunt the unstoried names
> of African Nairobi, where by Nyanza's lakes
> Nile hid his flooding fountain, or in the New World
> far Pasadena's roseland, whence who saileth home
> westward wil in his kalendar find a twin day.
> But I in England starving 'neath the unbroken glooms
> of thatt dreariest November which wrapping the sun,
> damping all life, had robb'd my poem of the rays
> whose wealth so far had sped it, I long'd but to be
> i' the sunshine with my history; and the names that held
> place in my heart and now shall hav place in my line
> wer Avignon, Belcaire, Montelimar, Narbonne,
> Béziers, Castelnaudary, Béarn and Carcasonne,
> and truly I coud hav shared their fancy coud I hav liv'd
> among those glad Jongleurs, living again for me,
> and had joy'd with them in thatt liberty and good-will
> which men call toleration, a thing so stiff to learn
> that to sceptics 'tis left and cynics.

Here and there, in this book, you will fall, unex-
pectedly, upon fine touches of satire, satire recalling — perhaps meant to recall — the fourth book of
Lucretius. Some of Mr. Bridges' parenthetical observations are interesting; as, for example, the statement that nobody could either by science or by

aesthetic arrive at the judgment that women are more
beautiful than men — *that* might have come from
Schopenhauer. Again, when Mr. Bridges says plainly
that he rates the pleasure of Beauty "even above the
pleasur of Virtue," the reader experiences a shock of
mild surprise; we are always surprised when poetry
turns out not to be prim.

Of the fourth and last book, which should sum and
order all that has preceded, I find it difficult often to
understand the connexions. Yet it contains many
passages not inferior in beauty to the best passages of
the first two books. Such are, if I may venture to
specify, the paragraphs which describe the excava-
tions at Ur and Kish, the opening paragraph of the
discussion upon Pleasure, the passage upon the scent
of garden-flowers (full of a rich and Keats-like sen-
suosity), and all the last 240 lines of the book. These
all have a quality either of grace or of nobility which
it would be hard to match in the poetry of the last
fifty years. Let me guarantee these praises by reading
to you — and so making reluctantly an end of quota-
tion — not much above a dozen lines from a passage
which, since it deals with first love, might more properly have found a place in the third book. First love
Mr. Bridges calls man's "second vision" — the first
vision is the vision of Motherhood:

> And so mighty is this second vision, which cometh
> in puberty of body and adolescence of mind
> that, forgetting his Mother, he calleth it "first Love";
> for it mocketh at suasion or stubbornness of heart,
> as the oceantide of the omnipotent Pleasur of God,
> flushing all avenues of life, and unawares

by thousandfold approach forestalling its full flood
with divination of the secret contacts of Love, —
of faintest ecstacies aslumber in Nature's calm,
like thought in a closed book, where some poet long since
sang his throbbing passion to immortal sleep — with coy
tendernesses delicat as the shifting hues
that sanctify the silent dawn with wonder-gleams,
whose evanescence is the seal of their glory,
consumed in self-becoming of eternity;
till every moment as it flyeth, cryeth "Seize!
    Seize me ere I die! I am the Life of Life."

I deprecated the praise of this poem as a miracle of youthfulness. But if that praise is, for the reason I gave, misjudged, this passage at least makes the misjudgment easily intelligible. And it suggests a question to which I could wish that I knew, or could better guess, the answer. Nearer ninety than eighty, Mr. Bridges has given us the only great poem that has appeared in living memory. What are our young men doing? How much younger — and cleaner — this is than anything that any of them have attempted! Emerson has said somewhere that "we only believe as deep as we live." That we only write as deep as we live is, I suppose, a platitude. But I sometimes wonder whether poetry would not be better if the critics of it contented themselves with shouting its platitudes from the housetops. Only out of ourselves can we create beauty, out of some beauty and reasonableness in our lives. *The Testament of Beauty* beareth witness with me. When we throw up our hands, to think that Mr. Bridges wrote this poem at eighty-five, at least let us remember that he took eighty-five years to write it; that is, to live it.

METHODS OF CRITICISM
IN POETRY

I THINK it was Seneca who first said, what Ben Jonson and many others have said after him, that the critic of poetry must be himself a poet. I wish I had the learning which would enable me to try out the dictum by a wide survey of the history of criticism. Such meagre half-learning as I have suggests to me that Seneca said either too much or too little. If from a review of the great critical names with which I am most familiar I were disposed to draw any inference, really I think it would be that the critic of poetry must be a poet, but not a very good one. Aristotle, greatest of critics, wrote poetry, if a man can be said to write poetry who writes an Ode to Virtue. If he was a good poet, he was an unlucky one; for only the critics know that he was a poet at all. The elder Scaliger, once one of the authoritative names in European criticism, was not only a poet, but a prolific one. Yet unless it was the younger Scaliger, I do not know who ever thought his poetry good. Ben Jonson was a poet, Sidney was a poet. Like everyone else, I like everything about Sidney; and as much of Ben Jonson as is good for me. But for neither of them, I imagine, will anyone claim a place with the great poets of the world. Perhaps we have not had many better critics than Dryden. We have had worse poets; yet if the critic of poetry must be a poet, but not a very good one, who better fills the bill than Dryden? A book that I feel I can never enough praise is Samuel Johnson's *Lives of the Poets*. Even so, to know that Dr. Johnson was not a great poet you need not go to his poetry, you may stay with the *Lives*. The more I read the other critics, and the more I discover how easy it is to be dull, the more does a judgment too personal to be wrong incline me to regard Hazlitt as the greatest of English critics. Hazlitt did not write poetry — how could he? He was consummate in a species which he was doomed not to write, but to live — tragi-comedy. Yet in early life he painted pictures; an art more difficult than poetry, for you cannot practise it till you have qualified. He painted pictures, but not first-class pictures: he was a painter, but not a very good one. To think of Hazlitt is to think of Coleridge; and not to know what to think. But I cannot think with the crowd about him. The appeal of his poetry is strong with me; and the appeal of the man. But just those qualities which make a critic, he seems to me to lack. Many persons, perhaps most, would give the first place in English criticism, not to Hazlitt, but to Matthew Arnold. To Matthew Arnold I cannot refuse the full title of a poet; and if I place him as a critic below Hazlitt, I do so doubtfully and half-ashamedly. But he became a great critic (I have said before) only when he had already ceased in effect to be a great poet. As a critic, he was much influenced by Sainte-Beuve, one of the greatest of critics and — a poet, but not a very good one.

If the best critics have been, for the most part, poets of the second rate, the poets of the first rate have, as often as not, when they have gone from poetry to the criticism of it, proved singularly poor critics. Goethe must rank, I suppose, as the greatest European poet of the nineteenth century. Yet has not Swinburne called him, in effect, the world's worst critic? — and cited chapter and verse for it? Take again Victor Hugo. When M. Anatole France wishes to shew that there is no such thing as criticism, but only liking and disliking, it is from Hugo that he fetches his most effective illustration — Hugo who, he says, was "utterly wrong in his judgments upon all the great classics, save one": a worse crime surely than never being right at all. Byron, who to Goethe, and to his own age, seemed a poet not inferior to Shakespeare — Byron uttered upon almost all the poets judgments preposterous beyond belief. Scott could be relied on to think almost any poetry good; conversely, Wordsworth had a way of thinking even the best poetry bad — if he had not written it himself. Of all these great poets, of course, the judgments which they make upon other poets, or upon poetry, are interesting, are worth having; but mostly, I think, as illustrations of moral temper, and not as criticism. The best criticism of other poets which a poet ever gives you is his own poetry.

The enemies of criticism — a tribe only less numerous than the enemies of truth — have found here material for their malice. If a great poet does not know what poetry is, who does?

Why, a good critic, I am disposed to answer. And really, is not that what you would expect? To set a poet to catch a poet, or a thief to catch a thief, is to forget the master quality in both temperaments. There would be no thieves, and we should all of us be policemen, were it not that human nature loves excitement and hates to patrol a "beat." The great poets are bad critics because they are too excitable. I will not say that the birth of a critic is the death of a poet; but it is, I think, his suspended animation. And you may know the great poet by the fact that he never suspends his animation.

I have mentioned policemen; and perhaps I had better not have done so. That there are laws of poetry I am still old-fashioned enough to believe. And if you are to have laws, you need, no doubt, policemen and judges and a legislature. That function of criticism which consists in patrolling the streets of literature is discharged, I suppose, by the journalists and reviewers. I should think better of it, perhaps, than I do if I were a better journalist. I appreciate in it the element of the *burly*, and whatever it may have of a large good-nature. I do not like to see the play of its truncheon too earnest. A more exalted conception of the critic figures him as a judge. If he must be a judge, and try poets, by preference let him try them, not for doing something wrong, but for doing something right. Yet again, we suppose the greatest critics of all, the Aristotles and the Scaligers, to be a kind of legislators. But they can only enact those laws that are given to them; they can only echo what was uttered on Sinai — out of great cloud.

A great many persons, I daresay most, have long since persuaded themselves that there are in fact no laws of poetry. There are no laws of poetry, because they are so often violated. By the same token, there are no Ten Commandments. Asked what he thought of the Ten Commandments as a moral code, a witty undergraduate wrote (under stress of examination) that, in his opinion, "Candidates should attempt Number 7, and at least four others." Well, the laws of poetry are so numerous that some of them will always be too much for the poet—or he for them. If the poet proves too much for the laws, they are changed. But that is true of the laws of England — perhaps even of the United States — equally with the laws of poetry. When the laws of poetry are changed, the critic, of course, has to begin again; the judiciary must administer what the legislature enacts.

But is this what we mean when we speak of the laws of poetry? Do we not rather mean that poetry has laws, not such as a state has, but laws which are like those of nature?

Here is one of those distinctions which seem more obvious than they are. Human laws change, the laws of nature are unchanging and eternal. That is much less true than we think it, or true in a different sense from that in which we commonly take it. When we change a human law, a law of the state, what takes place is, not properly a change of law, but a readjustment of the human mind and of human behaviour to newly revealed conditions of the political or moral life, to a new conception of law. The divorce laws, for example, do not change the law of marriage; they merely readjust our ideas about it. In just the same way Copernicus readjusted our ideas of the planetary system; he did not change the laws of astronomy.

I suppose, then, that there are laws of poetry which are so far like the laws of nature that our best expression of them is in any period imperfect, our formulas requiring readjustment as our experience widens and deepens. I think of them none the less as real laws, in respect of which we are, I sometimes fancy, actually better situated than in respect of those laws which express our knowledge of the external world. Does not history itself suggest that the laws of poetry are better ascertained than those of nature? Take the history of poetry from Homer to Housman; and compare with it the history of any science over a like term of centuries. Take astronomy and physics as they were for Thales and Anaximander. Think then of Newton and Einstein. Is not the measure of difference a new heaven and a new earth? Our conception of the world of poetry seems, in comparison, to have changed hardly at all.

It is not difficult to divine the reason of this. Poetry is what it is because from the beginning it answers to a spiritual need in man. It expresses human desire. It develops by way of our wants. Nature, on the other hand, has no alliance with our desires, she cares nothing for what we want: indeed her best aim seems often used to baffle both our desires and our calculations.

I say all this because the criticism of poetry is too much thought of, and spoken of, as though it were, from the very nature of its material, an art essentially whimsical and capricious. The truth is that we attend too much to the occasional perplexities of criticism, and too much forget what a solid and impressive body of agreed opinion there is about the best poetry. Every now and again a great poet, as Wordsworth, will tell you that a great poem, for example, Gray's *Elegy*, is not poetry at all — "unintelligible" Wordsworth called it; yet a man might well be forgiven if he called it the only great poem in the world that everybody has understood. Occasionally a good critic will fall foul of a poet whom it becomes all the world to speak fair; a notable example is Matthew Arnold's depreciation of Shelley. But we allow these occasional *bêtises* to distract us more than they need. For in truth, is anything about poetry more marvellous than the fact that we nearly always agree upon it? We quarrel about history, we quarrel about science, we quarrel about what is much more important than either, religion. But we almost never quarrel about poetry; and when we do, it is not about the substance of it, it is about some accident of it; or it sometimes happens that, when we suppose ourselves to be talking about poetry, we are really talking about something else. What is the matter, for example, with Matthew Arnold's essay upon Shelley is, not that it is a bad essay on poetry, but that it is a good essay upon quite a different subject — respectability.

I cannot but feel that we look at criticism in too

fussy a spirit, not sufficiently appreciating its free-
doms and securities. It is well that the critic should
know his limitations. Yet I find a sensible comfort
in reflecting what wide unembarrassed tracts the
province of criticism in fact offers. We should be better critics, I fancy, if we more often thought of criticism as, over the far greater part of it, a field of infinite delight in which our talents and our ingenuities
may wander harmlessly. It is not often, it is not perhaps more than once in a century, that criticism runs
upon a crisis. There are laws of poetry just as there
are laws of the state. But we need not think of poetry,
or of life, too uncomfortably. It is not a normal condition, it is an exceptional condition, and not a
healthy one, to be conscious of the laws of the human
body. It is an exceptional and not a normal condition
to be wanting the police, to appeal to the courts, to
petition the legislature. The normal condition is one
which mixes with life upon far easier terms. The same
holds good of poetry and the laws of poetry. I do not
say that poetry might not be better than it is. But it is
not often in poetry that anybody does murder.

These are practical considerations; and I think it is
sometimes worth while not to look at criticism in too
metaphysical, or ultimate, a fashion. Criticism is, or
ought to be, one of the most delightful departments of
literature; and that is especially true of the criticism
of poetry. If I may speak of personal predilections, I
should be inclined to rank as the top literary pleasures, first, reading poetry, and secondly, reading
what has been written about poetry. And of what has

been written about poetry the best, all the world over, is, I cannot but think, what has been written *freest*, with the least worry of head, the least disposition to break the heart over ultimate questions. The laws of poetry are serviceable, not that the critic may forever be reminding us of them, but because, so secure are they, in the main, that he can afford to forget them. He can afford to indulge his temperament, he can allow himself infinite experiment, he can be a creature of likes and dislikes. Very rarely, after all, unless he deals with contemporary poetry, has he got to ask himself, of what he reads and comments upon, Is this poetry? Mostly, the question has been answered for him long since. The mere reviewer — I use the term without disparagement — the mere reviewer has to ask this question, he has to ask it too often, and to answer it too quickly. But it does not much matter. By the grace of God — and from the nature of his profession — he *always knows the answer*. Nature rarely tempts us beyond what we can bear; she gives us winter according to our wool, and assurance proportionate to the hurry we are in. I would add, in seriousness, that I marvel how well upon the whole the reviewer does his work. Incompetent reviewers are, in comparison with incompetent poets, rare. Nor would I, as some do, complain of reviewers that they too much aim at being clever. At least it is better than to aim at being dull. There are critics of poetry who take, I feel, more pains to be dull than truth is worth. The more I see of human dullness, the better I like a brisk journalism.

Indeed, when I ask what the aim is, or should be, of criticism or the critic, I am disposed to put first among critical duties that of being interesting and giving pleasure. Of course, there are the saints of criticism — I was speaking of one of them only last week. In Matthew Arnold the pose of impersonality is carried with such art that it would be absurd to withhold our admiration. If he passes judgment, it is not he that does it, but the *orbis terrarum*, the whole congregation of saints. For him criticism knows nothing of persons; nor poetry either — the poet has neither father nor mother, nor any place in the history of literature; or if he has, it is a kind of impertinence, and is not going to help him in the day of judgment. Well, it needs must be that there should be pontiffs; and perhaps it is their sufficient excuse if they succeed in being good art. Yet I think it better to look at criticism a little more naturally.

More than any other of the literary kinds, criticism approximates to a *social* art — and this may be why the poets are unsuccessful in it. It is the most natural thing in the world to discuss a book or a poem — far more natural than to write one. It is one of the most obvious of social acts or behaviours, but like any other social act it perishes in the defect of those qualities which afford pleasure and make a man interesting.

If I ask by what means a critic principally achieves his business of being interesting and giving pleasure, there are three virtues which seem to me, beyond any others, to come into question. They are: the range of his information, the variety of his method, and the emphasis of his personality. The range of his information should be this side of erudition — or the critic will perish in the historian; and this is, in any case, a social art, where the first of crimes is to be tiresome, to be a bore. More important for the critic than the range of his information is, I think, variety of method; and I do not know that he can have too much of it. Too many critics have only their pet method. There are those who favour, to the exclusion of all other methods, the exegetical method; the only service, they suppose, which a critic can perform for a poet is to explain the meaning of what he says. Other critics, feeling rather deeply that a poem is what it is just because the meaning of it does not admit statement in any other terms, suppose the only criticism to be the purely receptive — that which begins and ends in appreciation. This is the cooing and reciting school. Always, it is — or has — its own reward. It is supposed, again, that a poem is best understood out of the poet, that the living method is the biographical. Let us have a picture of the man in his habit as he lived. Or better still, let us psycho-analyse him. If we know his diseases, we shall find him, if not more intelligible, at any rate more interesting. Other critics seek to understand poetry, not out of the poet, but out of the political and social conditions of the age in which he lives. For these I shall have a special word presently. Nor must I forget the claims of the bibliographical method. "The future of Shakespeare," I read the other day, "lies with bibliography." I congratulated Shakespeare that he was a poet with a future; but I could have wished him gayer in his friendships.

Truth to tell, I like all these methods; and there are others, and I like to mix them. Some of them I like better than others; specially do I like to mix poetry with biography. Even so, I am not too fond of full-dress biography. The model here for literary criticism is, I think, Sainte-Beuve. But in general, variety seems to me a grace of criticism so obvious that I wonder it should be so little sought.

And lastly, there is the emphasis of personality. This is something to be valued, I have always thought, beyond all critical accomplishments. That is why I have that joy which I have in Hazlitt. In criticism, after all, we are talking about books — after men, the most interesting thing in the world; just because they are so interesting, literary criticism exists. An interested manner is vital. In the criticism of poetry, we are talking about the best books of all; and our tone will be pitched accordingly; the interested manner will take on, it may be, and if need be, something of spiritual accent. Poetry means something; and we cannot tolerate that a man should speak of it as though it did not mean something to *him*. We do not ask him to be aggressive, but we do, I think, demand that he should be personal, and we forgive him easily if he is intensely personal.

I say so much gaily and confidently. But I am aware that I may seem to say more than I mean. For I would not be thought to throw in my lot with

that school of literary metaphysic which reduces both
poetry and the criticism of poetry to self-expression.
For "schools" of criticism, generally, I have not
much liking — when they happen, I prefer to call
them cliques. They happen more in France than in
England. About America I do not know — about
America I have acquired a habit of not knowing. But
I have the suspicion that schools, whether of poetry or
of criticism, are mostly alien to the Anglo-Saxon
temper. However, so much do I value the emphasis of
personality, that I find myself immensely interested
in that school of criticism which styles itself the subjective. Indeed, if ever I wanted to join a school of
critics I think it would be this one. I should fail, I
know, to secure entrance; because I believe, I have
said, in laws of poetry. To do that is to be objective.
But in my heart I much better like the subjective
critics. I like their superior liveliness and plausibility;
the effort to be objective I sometimes feel to have in it
some fated element of dullness and donnishness. At
the moment, the subjective critics seem to be almost
everywhere in power; and much as I like them, their
vogue alarms me. I like them, but I fall short of be-
lieving in them. While of the personal element in
criticism I am ever so willing that anyone should
make a gospel, they have gone further than that, they
have made a metaphysic. Whether of their own
metaphysic they are more properly to be regarded as
the fanatics or the cynics, I am never quite sure.

I think it a faulty metaphysic; and such time as I
have left myself I propose to give to criticising it.

For a typical expression of their creed I will go to a writer whom I have already mentioned, M. Anatole France, taking from his *Vie Litteraire*[1] some sentences which are well known and, as we might expect, well pointed. "There is no such thing," says M. France, "as objective criticism, just as there is no such thing as objective art. Any man who is vain enough to think that he puts into his work anything except himself is the victim of a mocking illusion. The plain truth is, a man cannot get out of himself. . . . It is best, I think, to accept that situation with the best grace we can, and to confess that, when we have not the good sense to hold our tongues, what we talk about is always ourselves."

Literature and poetry, that is, and equally with both, criticism, begin and end in self-expression.

I like the liberating quality of that; and the wide room it gives to the play of personality in criticism. Yet as soon as I ask myself what is meant by self-expression, I see crowding in upon subjective criticism difficulties and perplexities of such magnitude and number that I begin to wonder whether it is not better, after all, to be dull and objective. Certainly, I can think of no brighter employment for youthful talent than that it should seek to express itself; and the adventure has the nobler lure when the poet or critic who affects self-expression has taken the pains to *be* something, to be somebody. It is a great thing to express anything at all; and when it comes to self-expression, I take it that even an uninteresting self,

[1] From the chapter on Jules Lemaître.

adequately expressed, and with truth and candour, is something near to the most interesting thing in the world. Yet when we speak of expressing ourselves, what do we in fact mean? I concede to the subjective critic that it is difficult to utter absolute truths, to express laws; the laws of poetry are not actual, they are a slowly self-realising ideal. But it is one thing, surely, to say that truth is partial and relative, another thing to say (what I understand the subjective critic to say) that it is personal. If the truths of poetry were personal, or its beauty personal, in what a garden of delight should we not all live, alike the makers of poetry and the appreciators of it and the critics! We should make, or we should take what was made; and it would be ours. Nothing else would matter. Nobody else would matter. In what a garden of delight should we not live — but how uselessly, and, in truth, how meaninglessly! For what is the matter with "self-expression," phrase and thing, is that it means nothing. It is easy to say that poetry is the personal reaction of a great poet upon the world, criticism the personal reaction of the critic upon the poet. But these personal reactions, so soon as you reflect upon them, are quickly discovered to be individual in a degree almost negligible, and in the main stuff of them hopelessly communal. Egoism as a literary theory is, in fact, open to all, and more than all, the objections which have been advanced against egoism as a moral or political theory. To persons who wish to be themselves, to think as they like, to do as they like — to all this wide class of libertines the just

rejoinder is "Let them try it." It cannot be done —
the world is not made like that. The world is not
made up of oneself and other people and things. The
contrast which we make between ourselves and other
people or other things, natural as, from habit, we
have come to think it, proceeds in fact from an artificial and, in some degree, sophistical reconstruction.
We can worry ourselves into awareness of it; but in
the normal health of the soul it does not obtrude itself. That is why egoistic theories of morality satisfy
nobody: selfishness is not the ultimate fact of human
nature. Nor is self-expression a primary element in
art. When I ask what I am, and attempt to answer
— when I essay, that is, self-expression — at once I
make two discoveries. First, I find myself compelled
to answer, or express myself, in terms, or words,
which are not my own, even for art, but which have
beauty or value only as part of an infinite tradition.
I find, I mean, that literature is so far not self-expression that it may more conveniently be conceived as a
kind of self-*com*pression — a compression of the stuff
of my individuality into forms of art, communal
forms in which I am at best but a managing partner.
Secondly, in every attempt which I make to express
myself, reflection drives me down upon a catalogue of
values or possessions in which I have, patently, no
proprietary rights. Wherein do the values of any of
us lie? — by our values I mean all that matters in us
and to us? My values lie in what I may call my
scene; in the manifold which is not myself; of which
the best part is, say, my friends and my books, or it

may be my fields; the things not mine in which I have laid up my heart. I am what I am not. As soon as I abstract myself from the environment, natural or human, which is the material of my thinking, I become aware how little, how nothing, I have, or am, which is my own.

Very few of us know how empty our minds are. Yet this spiritual vacuity is a kind of strength. We have no ideas of our own; we have nothing of our own to say. Alike in our worst falsehoods and our best paradoxes, we are merely accomplices with the world — we have that grand security, more than compensating the limitations involved. Similarly, even of the great poet, the prophesying soul expresses, not itself, but "the prophetic soul of the great world." It is a commonplace that the success of a stage-play depends quite as much upon the audience as upon the actors. The public acts the play — that is why we are never equal to Shakespeare. The public acts the play; and in a sense it writes it. Shakespeare's public was a mixed crowd; but it was good enough to write Shakespeare. We must suppose it, indeed, the most poetically minded audience that ever any poet addressed; a public consisting of lovers of eloquence, artists in declamation, specialists in all the arts of magnificence.

But once again I have begun to say more than I mean, or to seem to do so. If I am not happy with the subjective critics, the self-expressionists, neither am I with that school of criticism which would reduce the study of poetry to observation of the political and social conditions in which it arises, endeavouring to persuade us that there are no great poets, but only representative ones. Apart from the age in which a poet is placed, there is, of course (as these critics allow), the age in which he lives; by which I mean the tradition of literature and history in which, from whatever accidents, he moves spiritually. It is not impossible for a Victorian poet — even, it may be, for a Georgian poet — to live, in respect of nine-tenths of him — the best of him, his poetry — in the age of Pericles. It is a useful occupation of criticism to study, so far as it admits study, the action upon a poet, of the conditions of his age. It is a useful occupation, and, I sometimes think, a more relevant one, to study the manner in which other ages, and the poetry of other ages, act upon him — after all, it were strange if poets did not learn more from poetry than they learn from the world. Both these occupations are pursued under obvious disabilities. Necessarily information is imperfect; and there is the chance that not merely some of our inferences, but our whole method of inference, may be wrong. We can never know, I mean, how far logical concepts are valid in the interpretation of that very special experience which poetry is. If I had to write a creed for the critic of poetry, the which except he hold he cannot possibly be saved, the first clause of it would be "I believe in the inspiration of poets . . ." Yet if there is such a thing as inspiration, the processes of it are, I cannot but suppose, different from those of logical deduction. Most of our criticism is, I suspect, ultimately sceptical; when we call poets "inspired," we use the term as a kind of courtesy title. We mean no more by it than we mean when we speak of the Bible as "written by God." If the Bible were written by God, it is remarkable that nobody reads it. Our criticism is bad because we are so miserably unbelieving. For myself, I have never found it hard to believe in the inspiration of poets, and it grows easier with me every day. I find it hard to think of poetry as self-expression; and I find it hard to think of it as the mere impression of the world upon the poet. Habitually, I think of environment as acting, not upon, but in and with, the poet — I conceive the poet, not as having, but as being, his experience. But of the assumption that he is acted upon by his conditions — and merely representative of them — I am not sure that the grand oversight does not lie in a misconception of what I will call the *reach* of the conditions. The poet is acted upon by, and represents, it is supposed, only actualised conditions — whether the actualisation be present or past. "The prophetic soul of the great world dreaming on things to come" is allowed to count for nothing. Yet the primary fact about poetry is that fact means nothing to it. Though it seems like poetry to say so, nothing, for poetry, happens in time. If it did, poetry would be history. The experience which poetry, or the poet, *is* (*is*, and not *has*), stands out of time. It is an experience, moreover, in which the distinction between expression and impression has no part; in which the form and the matter of thought, or imagination, are, not two things, but a single effect.

I hate to say things hard and mystical. But in truth I find no difficulty in supposng that the world-consciousness which speaks in poetry is a consciousness before and after. How indeed could this slowly self-realising world-consciousness ever be realised at all unless the end of its mystery stirred already in its initial and middle processes? That, in fact, is what makes it possible to speak of the laws of poetry at all, and to think of them as living entities.

Just now I was commending those pleasant places of criticism where a man might walk without fear of metaphysic. And before I know where I am, I find myself trespassing on the world to come. I am not sure that the fault lies with me; I am inclined to lay it to the account of the subject. Is it, perhaps, in the very nature of poetry that hardly has a man begun to speak of it than he loses himself in speculations about life everlasting?